Unleash Your Inner Renegade

DISRUPT THE BULLSHIT STORY YOU KEEP TELLING YOURSELF + UPLEVEL YOUR LIFE

A WORKBOOK FOR GROWTH
BY LOTUS BANKS

UNLEASH YOUR INNER RENEGADE

Unleash Your Inner Renegade

© Copyright 2025 by Lotus Banks.

All rights reserved. No part of this book may be copied, reproduced, stored, shared, or transmitted in any form or by any means — electronic, mechanical, photocopying, recording, or otherwise — without prior written permission from the author.

This includes but is not limited to **any portion of the book, exercises, frameworks, methodologies, or original concepts.** Unauthorized use, duplication, or distribution of this material without express permission is a direct violation of copyright law.

All content is original to **Lotus Banks** unless otherwise noted.

Cover Design by Erin Morgan
ISBN: 978-0-578-83462-7

For more info, coaching, certifications, and other badassery, visit:
 www.TheLotusBanks.com

🔥 DISCLAIMER 🔥

This workbook is meant for **informational and inspirational** use only. The author is **not** a doctor, therapist, or scientist, and nothing in these pages is intended to **diagnose, treat, or cure any condition**—mental, physical, or otherwise.

By choosing to read and apply any content from this book, you **acknowledge and agree** that any decisions or changes you make—mentally, physically, emotionally, financially, or otherwise—are **100% your responsibility**. The author assumes **zero liability** for any outcomes, perceived or actual, from your use of this material.

If you have (or suspect you have) a **medical or psychological** condition, please consult a **qualified** health professional. This workbook is designed to **spark self-reflection, awareness, and growth** — not to replace the professional support you may need and deserve.

💡 **In other words:** I'm sharing my **personal experiences, strategies, and perspectives** to help you wake the hell up to your own power. Take what resonates, leave what doesn't, and — most importantly — seek proper help whenever needed.

Stay bold. Stay safe. Stay disruptive.

UNLEASH YOUR INNER RENEGADE

Dedication

My poppa, for all the times you let me talk for hours about all things NLP, mindset, therapy, neurotransmitters, brain/gut, mind/body, quantum weirdness, and the list goes on.

My momma, for truly being my #1 fan since forever.

Sasha, for truly having you in my life for the first time.

Jean, for reconnection, forgiveness, grace, and acceptance.

Kyle, for showing me what healed masculine energy looks, sounds, and feels like.

Tatjana, Jordi, Alyssa, Heather, Tav, Tammy – there aren't enough words to describe my immense gratitude for your personal support in 2023.

Charles + George - for your impact on my life.

Erin, for everything in the OG days of ideation, and for all the times we laughed over everything and nothing.

Kipp, Clint, Jaime, and Tina - for introducing me to personal development.

To **all of you**, the readers, for having Bold Willingness™ to buy this book because you're ready to *disrupt the bullshit!*

Thank you for believing in **you**.

Thank you for believing and trusting in me to be your guide.

I love you immensely.

Contents

INTRODUCTION		PAGE 9
LEVEL 1:	PREPARE FOR DISRUPTION	PAGE 12
LEVEL 2:	CIRCLE OF CLARITY™	PAGE 18
LEVEL 3:	CAUSE AND EFFECT	PAGE 24
LEVEL 4:	BOLD ZONE BLUEPRINT™	PAGE 30
LEVEL 5:	MODEL OF REALITY	PAGE 38
LEVEL 6:	STATE MANAGEMENT	PAGE 48
LEVEL 7:	EFFORT TO ENERGY	PAGE 56
LEVEL 8:	FORM OF INTELLIGENCE	PAGE 64
LEVEL 9:	BREATHE	PAGE 70
LEVEL 10:	RELEASING LIMITING BELIEFS	PAGE 76
LEVEL 11:	FOUR GEARS TO INITIATE PROGRESS™	PAGE 84
LEVEL 12:	PADRR™	PAGE 94
LEVEL 13:	MIRROR, MIRROR	PAGE 104
LEVEL 14:	VISUALIZE YOUR FUTURE	PAGE 112
LEVEL 15:	NOW WHAT?	PAGE 122
CLOSING + CONNECTING		PAGE 131

Introduction

Let me just say — **hell yes, you're here!**

Whatever pulled you to this workbook, **trust it**. You are **exactly** where you're meant to be. Inside these pages isn't just some collection of self-help fluff, it's a **reckoning**. A call to break free from everything that's been running the show in the background of your life. Oh! And that **something extraordinary** you've been searching for? **It's not out there.** It's already within you… just waiting for permission to be **unleashed**.

This workbook is your **opportunity for disruption** – the kind that rewires your mind, annihilates your patterns, and strips away every outdated belief that's been keeping you stuck. **This is personal evolution in real-time.**

Consider these pages your **safe space**, not in the coddling sense, but in the **"this is where you get radically honest with yourself"** sense. Here, you'll uncover the subconscious programming that's shaped your life. You'll confront it, challenge it, and then? **Decide what gets to stay, what gets burned to the ground, and what gets rewritten.**

At the end of every level, you'll find introspective questions designed to take you **deeper than you've ever gone before**. These aren't just questions, they're catalysts. They're the doorway to **who you've always been capable of becoming.**

Here's the deal: This workbook will **meet you at the exact depth** you are willing to go. So, I'm challenging you right now to unleash your inner renegade and…

- 💥 Be more honest with yourself than ever before.
- 💥 Be more vulnerable with yourself than ever before.
- 💥 Be more open with yourself than ever before.

Be bold. Be willing. Be seeking.

Because the version of you who isn't weighed down by all the old conditioning? **They're waiting for you on the other side of this.** 😊

xo, Lotus

RENEGADE | ren· e· gade | renəˌgād | noun
When an otherwise civilized human **breaks free from their norm, smashes societal expectations, and reclaims their damn power** without giving two fucks about convention.

UNLEASH YOUR INNER RENEGADE

📣 **Let's Stay Connected — Your Breakthroughs Matter!**

I wonder how many ways you're about to start **seeing yourself differently**? How many moments in the coming days will prove that your **transformation is already in motion**, even before you fully realize it?

🚀 **Go on a treasure hunt**, every single day, looking for evidence that you're already shifting, thinking differently, and stepping into something bigger.

And when those moments hit? **I want to hear all about them.**

💥 Your expanded awareness.
💥 Your mindset shifts.
💥 Your holy-shit-I-see-it-now breakthroughs.
💥 Your moments of **pure, undeniable transformation.**

Because this isn't just about reading a book. **This is about becoming.**

📩 **Email me:**
Hello@TheLotusBanks.com

📱 **Tag me on FB & Insta:**
@Lotus.Banks

🔥 Your success starts the moment you decide. Let's celebrate it together.

> "Until you make the subconscious conscious, it will direct your life and you will call it fate."

CARL JUNG

Level One

PREPARE FOR DISRUPTION

You think disruption happens only when life slams you to the ground and forces you to crumble. But what if disruption could be your most powerful ally? What if you had the audacity to **choose** it, **invite** it in, and let it propel you forward? This kind of disruption is intentional, courageous, and laser-focused on serving your future self. It's gritty. It's about building the emotional and physical capacity you say you crave, so when life does knock you down, you don't just get back up — you rise with the capacity to **be** more, **do** more, **have** more, and **give** more.

In this first level, I want you to embrace the idea that growth isn't accidental. It's an *intentional disruption* of everything that isn't serving you. Because when you disrupt the bullshit holding you back (and let's be real—**it's *all* bullshit**), you step out of the audience seat and onto the stage of your own life. You stop waiting for permission to transform. You become the living, breathing proof that you can burn away the old story and rise even stronger, like a phoenix choosing its own flames. There's pain in the burning, sure, but there's also rebirth on the other side.

That's the real difference between *change* and *progress*. Change is inevitable. The whole world and everything around us is always changing. Progress, though? That's a conscious choice. That's you being bold, willing, and seeking as you uncover and dismantle every bullshit belief and outdated unresourceful pattern of behavior that no longer serves you. Progress demands you stare your old behaviors in the face and say, "No more. I'm done letting this run me!" You go deeper, beneath the surface-level fluff, and dig up the roots of who you are, who you've been pretending you can't be, and who you never fucking were in the first place.

This level is all about lighting that initial spark of awareness. Instead of fearing the crumble, *activate* it! Because once you disrupt what's no longer aligned, you clear space for something far more potent. And remember: you're not aiming for perfection (spoiler alert—it doesn't exist). You're unleashing the part of you that's bold enough to tear down walls and audacious enough to reshape your reality.

This is your "Prepare for Disruption" moment. The start of a journey where you rewrite your rules, rebuild your mindset, and come out the other side with the unshakable knowing that you've got this, no matter what life throws at you.

But why go through all this? Because you deserve to experience the version of you that doesn't take crap from outdated beliefs, that doesn't wait for permission to evolve, and that refuses to stay stuck. This isn't about "fixing" anything that's wrong; it's about *activating* everything that's right, your inherent power, vision, and boldness. Think of the payoff: how would it feel to break free from the cycles and habits that have held you back, to replace old excuses with fresh possibilities, and to wake up every morning knowing you're taking steps toward an upgraded life?

What's that experience worth? Picture yourself realizing that every choice you make, every shift you allow, cements a new reality. It's not just about getting rid of the bullshit; it's about letting something stronger and more aligned take its place. Suddenly, you're not dreading Monday morning or avoiding difficult conversations; you're facing them head-on, because you *know* you can handle it. That's freedom.

That's the **life-shifting** reward of "intentional disruption."

Right here, right now.

If you're willing to push through the discomfort and step into the unknown, you open up a world where old limits no longer apply. This level isn't just a starting point; it's the foundation for every bold move you'll make from here on out. The question is: do you value your growth enough to invest in the temporary chaos of transformation? If your answer is yes, **hell yes**, then you're right where you're meant to be. **Let's.Fucking.Go.**

Intentional Disruption

Take the time to dive deep. Remember, awareness is the spark, action is the fuel. Now's your chance to set the tone for all the levels that follow. Go all in. You've got this!

What areas of my life feel stagnant, and why am I choosing to stay there?

_____
_____
_____
_____
_____
_____

How is fear of judgement, failure, or loss preventing me from seeing the potential in <u>choosing</u> intentional disruption?

_____
_____
_____
_____
_____
_____

If I gave myself permission to crumble *by choice,* like the phoenix burning itself, what might I discover about my hidden strengths?

_____
_____
_____
_____
_____

Notes For Integration:

"If you restore balance in your own self, you will be contributing immensely to the healing of the world."

DEEPAK CHOPRA

Level Two

CIRCLE OF CLARITY™

Picture trying to drive an old, outdated vehicle with a broken gas gauge. That's what it feels like when one major area of your life is running on fumes. Sure, you might still move, but you'd never know how much is left in your tank. When a part of your life feels broken and isn't operating at its full potential, it can feel so daunting to fix, that you disconnect, avoid, or hit the 'fuck it' button altogether. It's like breaking down in the middle of nowhere and having no clue where to go for help. That sense of overwhelm often locks you into the very patterns you're trying to disrupt.

Taking the time to assess where you stand right *now* is the first step towards intentional progress. **You can't fix what you can't see, and you can't disrupt what you refuse to acknowledge.**

Enter the Circle of Clarity™: A quick visual that helps you gauge six key areas of your life: **Personal Growth, Physical Body, Professional Growth, Fun & Leisure, Wealth,** and **Connection.**

Here's how it works:
1. **Review the Circle of Clarity**™ and rate each area of life from 1 to 10. This is an awareness tool, not a judgement. Rate it from one (emptier than a gas tank on E) to ten (straight-up aligned and thriving). Go!
2. Now, notice the areas where running on empty (or close to it). If your finances are a 2 while your career is a 9, you might be hustling so hard, that you're ignoring your money mindset or spending habits. If your physical body is a 10, and your personal growth is a 1, you might be spending so much time making the outside look good while ignoring what's going on inside you.

When you tune in and expand your awareness, now you finally have the power to do something about it. If you want to live with Bold Willingness™, you've <u>got</u> to stay honest with yourself about where you are, and hungry for where you want to be.

<u>Side Note:</u> I always recommend revisiting your circle (and doing a fresh rating) at least twice a year to track your evolution. Each time you do, you'll see new opportunities for growth and maybe even a few zones you've leveled up without realizing it.

UNLEASH YOUR INNER RENEGADE

Circle of Clarity ™

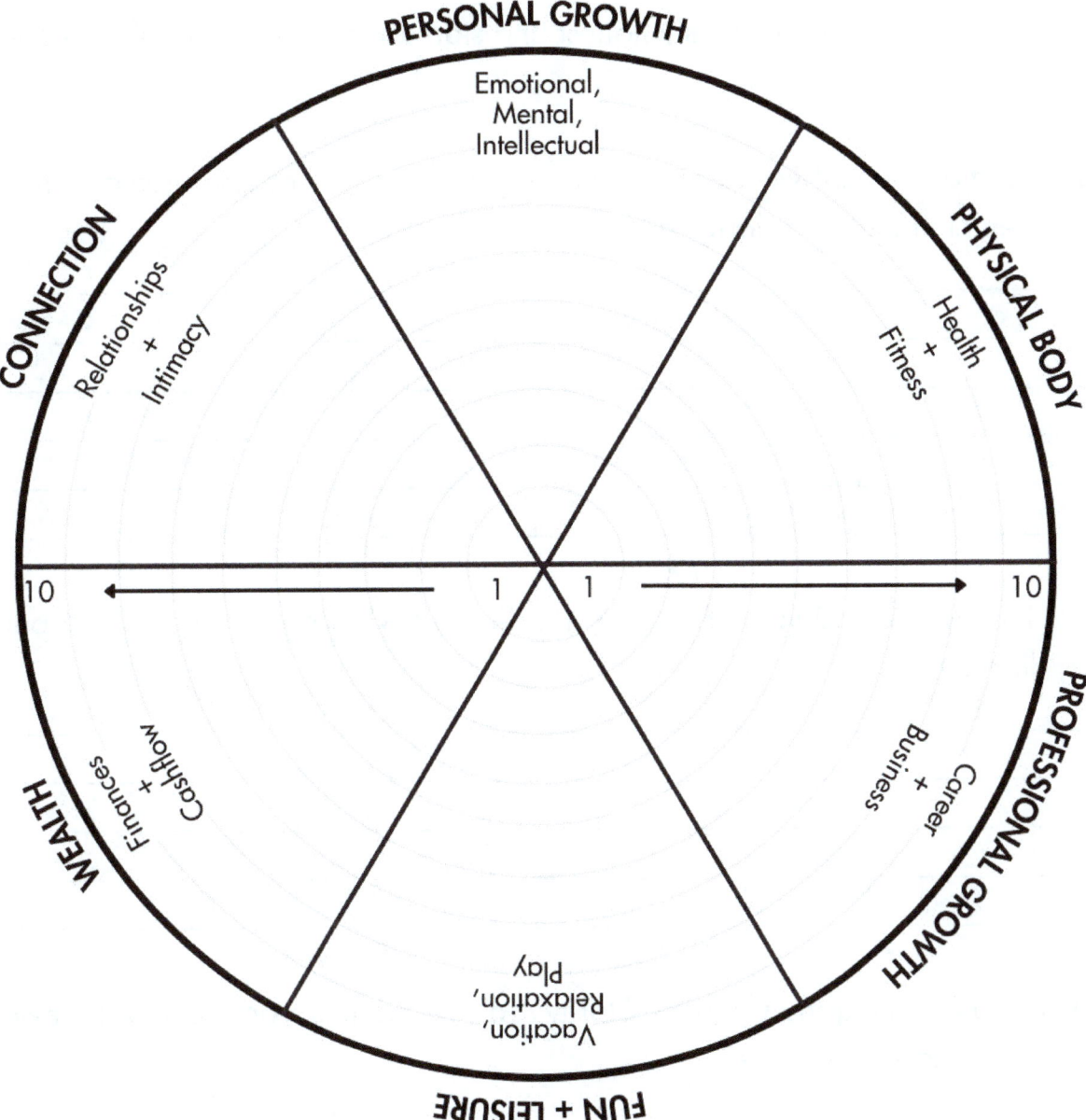

Trust your gut, and rate each area of your life between 1-10
1 = Almost Empty
10 = Totally Aligned, Fulfilled + Killin' it!

Renegade Reflection:

Use these questions as a deep-dive exploration of where you are and where you're going. Give yourself the space to be radically honest and start taking ownership of your life. You've got this!

Which area's improvement would bring me the greatest sense of joy, momentum, or relief, and why haven't I made it a priority yet?

_____
_____
_____
_____
_____
_____

Where am I stuck in avoidance or 'fuck it' mode, and what do I think will happen if I do something different?

_____
_____
_____
_____
_____

If I committed to revisiting my Circle of Clarity™ a few months from now, what evidence of progress would I most love to see?

_____
_____
_____
_____
_____
_____

Notes For Integration:

"The victim mindset dilutes the human potential. By not accepting personal responsibility for our circumstances, we greatly reduce our power to change them."

STEVE MARABOLI

Level Three

CAUSE AND EFFECT

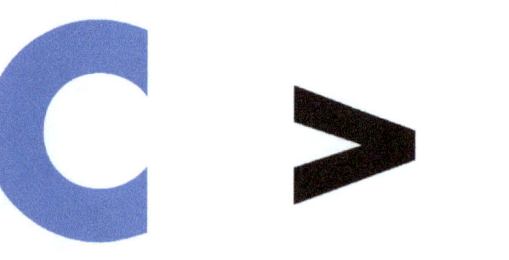 

CAUSE	**EFFECT**
(AT) CAUSE	**(IN) EFFECT**
RESPONSIBILITY	**VICTIM**
RESULTS	**REASONS**

Do you ever feel like life's dragging you around in the mud? Like no matter what you do, something or someone keeps getting in your way? That's called living in effect. It's that mindset of "I can't make progress because my boss sucks/my partner won't listen/I don't have the money." But here's the deal: The more you fixate on the reasons you **can't**, the more you stay stuck. The moment you decide to own your results and live **at cause**, everything changes. You shift your neurology, open new possibilities, and step back into the power you've been giving away.

Why is this so important? Because if you're the problem, then **you are also the solution**. There is nothing more empowering than realizing you hold the key to your own freedom.

Living **at cause** means taking responsibility for everything you create in your life: the good, the bad, and the "holy shit, did I really do that?!" Living **in effect** means letting outside forces decide your results. **It's victim mode**. One big laundry list of excuses, reasons, rationalizations, and bullshit. Now, being at cause doesn't guarantee life will always be "good", easy, or fair. It does, however, guarantee that you're the one calling the shots.

When you live at cause, you are the one responsible for getting your results. Live in effect, and you'll get all the reasons and excuses as to why you don't have the life that you say you want. It's like that quote from Arnold Schwarzenegger, "You can have results or excuses, not both." My version of that is, "Your choice. Results or Reasons. Not both."

So how do we decipher which side of the formula we've been living on? More importantly, once we become aware, what do we do with that information then?

Here's the process:

1. **Spot the Symptoms**: Pick one area in your life that's on life support. Ask yourself, "Where am I blaming someone/something else for my lack of progress?" This is where you're living in effect.

2. **Flip the Script**: Take responsibility for your results, now! No more victimhood. What if you decided, just for a day, that every result in that area was yours to own? See how that shift in perspective feels? Now, you and you alone hold the key and have the power to own your future.

3. **Ask Better Questions**: Move from "Why is this happening to me?" to "How did I create this, and what can I learn?" Watch your mind shift into solution mode.

So, what if you went all-in and lived at cause? You'd be the person who sees obstacles not as reasons to quit but as signals for growth. You'd create momentum in every area of your life because now you're focused on what you **do** want, rather than what you don't. You'd expand your sphere of influence, reminding people around you that if **you** can do it, so can they. And there's power in that. Real, unstoppable power.

You'd go on to create everything you want in life (and likely more) as you would be moving toward a more fulfilling, more exciting future. Which, by the way, usually lies outside of our Comfort zone. 😉

Renegade Reflection:

Dare to cause an effect *within* yourself, right now. Know that you may need to come back to this level to remind yourself of the power that lies in choosing to live at cause, why you're here, and why you **must** stay committed to this process. Because once you own your life, nothing, and no one, can take that power away.

Where in my life have I been secretly blaming someone or something outside of me for my outcomes?

_____
_____
_____
_____
_____
_____

What if I saw every challenge as an opportunity to test my commitment to living at cause, how would I respond differently?

_____
_____
_____
_____
_____

What's one immediate action I can take today to prove to myself (and my subconscious mind) that I'm done living in effect?

_____
_____
_____
_____

Notes For Integration:

"In any given moment we have two options, to step forward into growth, or to step back into safety."

ABRAHAM MASLOW

UNLEASH YOUR INNER RENEGADE

Level Four

BOLD ZONE BLUEPRINT™

UNLEASH YOUR INNER RENEGADE

Bold Zone Blueprint™

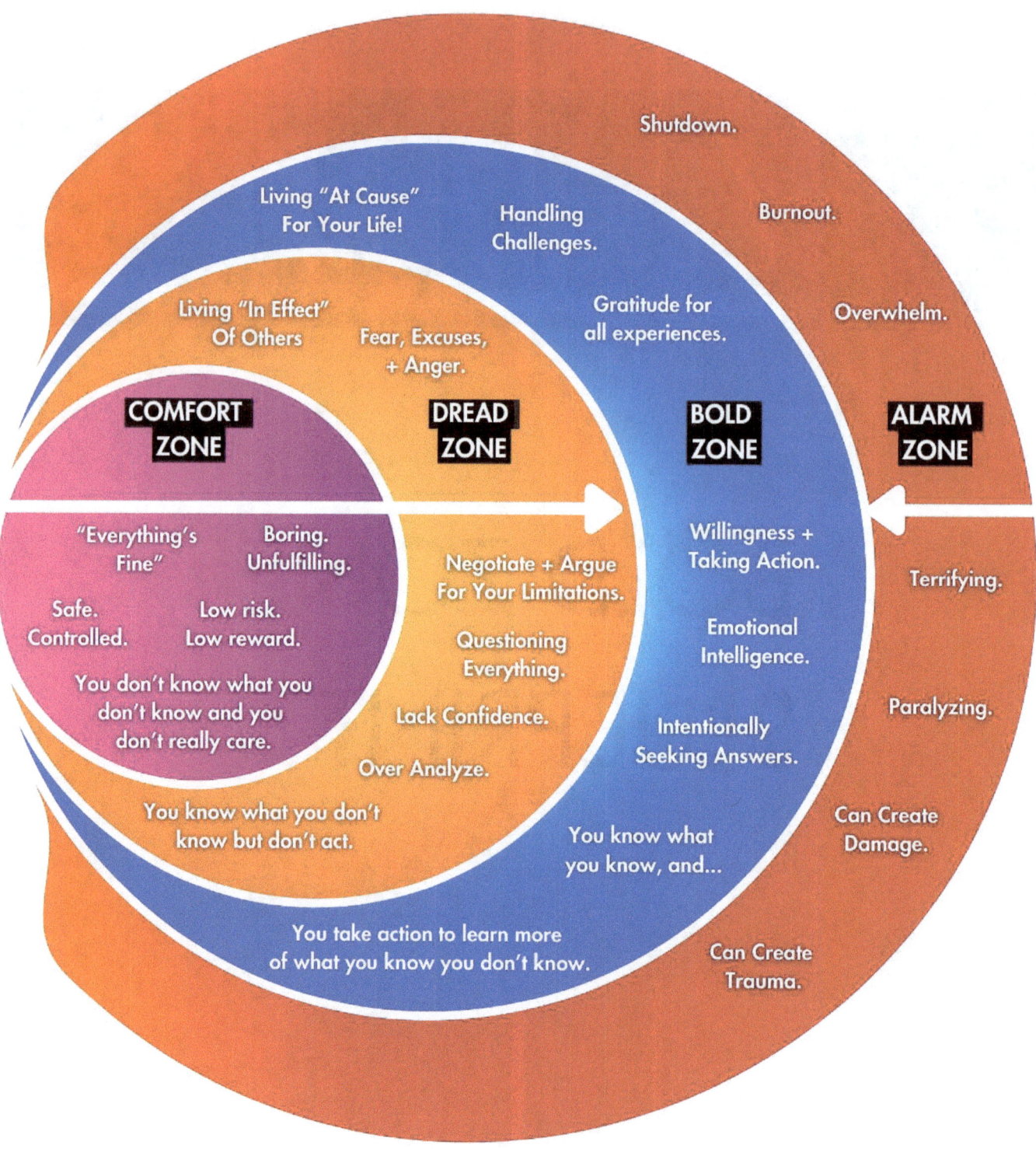

Have you ever noticed your life feels like it's on autopilot? Now I know that might feel safe and predictable, yet, isn't it also unfulfilling? That's because 'autopilot' is your **Comfort Zone**. It's your subconscious mind whispering to you, "Stay here. Don't rock the boat. Stay in that safe, familiar zone where nothing ever changes." You are wired to stay here, even if that familiarity means a stagnant, limiting, or downright miserable life. Living on repeat might keep you "safe," but it also keeps you small. And you're here because you refuse to stay small for **one.more.damn.day.** Right?!

True growth begins the moment you decide you're done playing by your old rules. That's where the **Bold Zone Blueprint**™ comes in. This visual and mental framework shows you the four zones you cycle through in life: Comfort, Dread, Bold, and Alarm. It's important to note that the amount of time you spend in each zone is different each year, each month, and each day.

The idea is to continue to expand your conscious awareness. Tuning in more frequently to which zone you're in (at that moment) and using it as a compass so you can gauge what to do next. Think of it like a map for your mind and behaviors, a cheat sheet to help you recognize where you stand, where you're headed, and where you need to shift.

Here's a quick rundown of each zone:

Comfort Zone
- You feel like "everything's fine" or maybe a bit bored. It's low risk, low reward.
- You don't know what you don't know, and you don't really care.
- Your subconscious mind thinks this is "safe," but safe here often means *stuck or unresourceful.*

Dread Zone
- The first place you land when you dare to step out of Comfort. Fear, excuses, and anger love to hang here.
- You know what you don't know, but you're not acting on it.
- You're stuck in resistance, overthinking, or living in effect instead of at cause.

Bold Zone
- The sweet spot of growth. You see challenges as opportunities to evolve.
- You know what you know, and you *take action* to learn more of what you don't.

- Emotional intelligence, willingness, and your relentlessly seeking spirit thrive here. This is where you unleash that badass, unstoppable version of you.

Alarm Zone
- If you go too far, too fast, or life sideswipes you, you can slam right into overwhelm, shutdown, and burnout.
- Your nervous system freaks out because it hasn't had this experience yet, it hasn't integrated the new behaviors or patterns you're creating, or you went too far, too fast.
- Recognize it quickly, then step back into the Bold Zone so you can keep building momentum without creating damage.

Now, what would happen if you fully committed to living in the Bold Zone as often as possible? You'd see life not as a threat, but as a playground for possibility. You'd harness the power of your subconscious mind, turning old fears into opportunities.

"But Lotus, what happens if I overstep and hit Alarm?" No biggie. Don't judge it. Notice it. Tune in, and see what's needed so you course correct and come back stronger.

When you recognize that you're not stuck, you're just <u>choosing</u> to stay in or out of these zones, you reclaim your freedom. You take your power back. You become the self-aware renegade who decides, moment by moment, to go boldly toward that future self you've been dreaming of.

Renegade Reflection:

Brace yourself: This level isn't just about naming zones; it's about claiming how you show up in each zone and deciding to stay **bold** for the long haul. Let's get it!

Where in my life am I bored or feeling "fine," and what does staying in Comfort cost me long-term?

_____
_____
_____
_____
_____
_____

Where and when have I felt the thrill of being in the Bold Zone™, and what beliefs helped me stay there?

_____
_____
_____
_____
_____
_____

How can I gauge when I'm drifting into Alarm, and what self-care or boundary-setting might pull me safely back to Bold?

_____
_____
_____
_____
_____

Notes For Integration:

📣 **Let's Stay Connected — Your Breakthroughs Matter!**

I wonder how many ways you can already feel yourself **shifting**? How many moments today will prove that your **transformation is already happening?**

🚀 **Go on a treasure hunt**, every single day, looking for evidence that you're already showing up differently, thinking differently, and seeing the world through a new lens.

And when you find those moments? **I want to hear all about them.**

💥 Your expanded awareness.
💥 Your mindset shifts.
💥 Your holy-shit-I-see-it-now breakthroughs.
💥 Your moments of **pure, undeniable transformation.**

Because this isn't just about reading a book. **This is about becoming.**

📧 **Email me:**
Hello@TheLotusBanks.com

📲 **Tag me on FB & Insta:**
@Lotus.Banks

💧 Your success is happening in real-time. Let's celebrate it together.

"When you change the way you look at things, the things you look at change."

WAYNE DYER

Level Five

MODEL OF REALITY

Have you ever caught yourself driving to work and suddenly realize you don't remember the entire trip? That's the power of your subconscious mind. Research suggests that **95%** of your daily thoughts, emotions, and actions happen on autopilot. Think of this as "old software" you don't even know exists. This means most of your life experience isn't shaped by conscious decisions, as your conscious mind only represents 5% of your reality. 95% of the reality you are experiencing on any given day is created by your automatic, default programming. This programming is based on the meaning you give to your childhood lessons, past experiences, and what was modeled to you by others.

You see, the subconscious mind's entire job is to "preserve the body". In order to achieve this, it will always choose whatever action it <u>perceives</u> as the "safest, most resourceful" option available at the time.

The challenge is that your subconscious mind doesn't think logically and is irrational. It processes life only in **pictures, sounds, and feelings.** Now, if the <u>meaning</u> you gave to those pictures, sounds, and feelings in your head are rooted in outdated beliefs, you'll keep repeating the same unresourceful patterns. Ever wonder why you can walk away from a situation feeling one way while someone else experiences it entirely differently? It's because we're each individually filtering millions of bits of information every second, that subconsciously shapes our <u>own</u> individual "truth."

To disrupt the bullshit story you've been telling yourself and actually create the future you want, you must first understand **how** <u>your</u> mind **creates** <u>your</u> reality. That's exactly what this level is about.

In NLP (Neuro-Linguistic Programming), this framework is often called the **Communication Model**; here, we'll refer to it as your **Model of Reality**. This framework reveals how your mind processes your external experience, giving <u>meaning</u> to what it **perceives** as important, then **projects** that back <u>out</u> to your reality.

UNLEASH YOUR INNER RENEGADE

Model of Reality

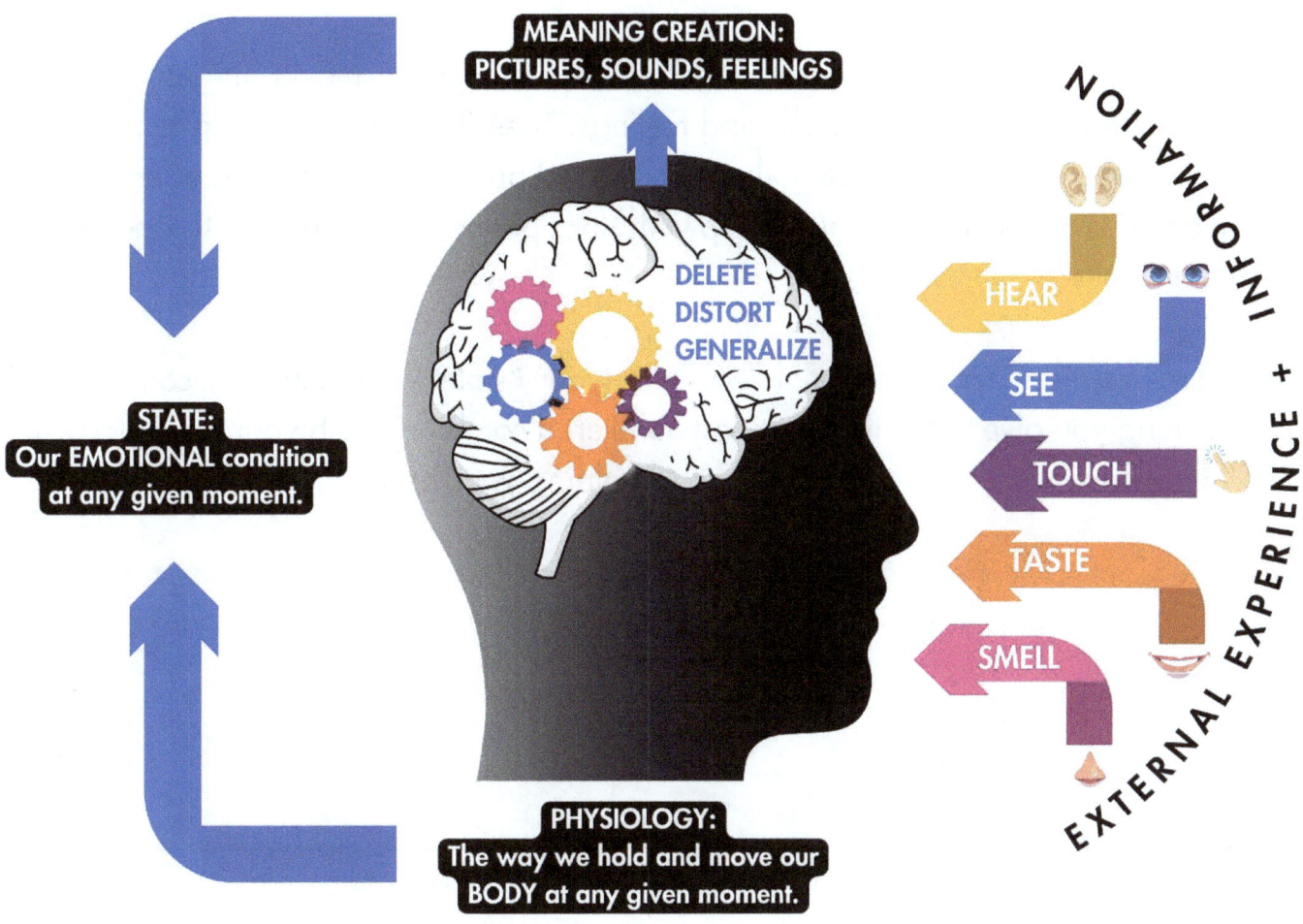

Picture this frame work like an assembly line:

1. **External Experience**: At any given moment, up to **2.3 million bits per second** (bps) of information assault your senses. *Example: The sight of your phone lighting up, the hum of the air conditioner, the subtle smell of coffee.* However, your conscious mind is only aware of **126 bits per second of information**. This is because of the filtering done by your subconscious mind.

2. **Filtering**: Your subconscious quickly **deletes** (ignores), **distorts** (twists), or **generalizes** (applies patterns) to that incoming information to fit your existing worldview. This filtering is driven by many things, some of which are: Your beliefs, past experiences, and emotional wiring. Then your subconscious mind serves up <u>only</u> the 126 bps it deems as most important for our conscious awareness.

3. **Meaning**: After filtering, your mind creates a mental movie in your head. A combination of pictures, sounds, and feelings. Then it assigns **<u>meaning</u>** to that mental movie based on the information that was filtered and your past life experiences. If that meaning is unresourceful, you end up with stuck patterns, limiting beliefs, and less than ideal results.

4. **State Creation**: Your emotional condition (your "state") is created by combining the meaning you give to the information you filtered combined with your physiology (how you're standing, breathing, moving, and holding your body).

    State Example: Slumped shoulders and shallow breathing? You'll likely feel low-energy or anxious. Upright posture and engaged breathing? You'll likely feel more confidence, more empowered.

I know this level can seem complex when first learned, so let's see this assembly line of processing with the following **real-life example on the next page:**

Imagine you're sitting in a team meeting. Your manager announces, "We need to discuss some concerns regarding the last project." Just as they say this, a coworker next to you exhales loudly and rolls their eyes.

External Event/Experience: coworker's sigh and eye-roll.

1. **Filtering**
    - Your subconscious mind instantly **deletes** most of the surrounding details: the dim lighting, the subtle buzzing of the AC, the fact that your coworker's having a stressful day.
    - It **distorts** what you do notice: maybe you interpret their eye-roll as a personal attack or a reflection on **your** performance.
    - It **generalizes**: perhaps you've seen eye-rolls before and assumed they always mean "I'm annoyed with you."
2. **Meaning**
    - Mental Movie Created:
        - **Picture**: In your mind, you see your coworker glaring at you (even if they didn't).
        - **Sound**: Your inner dialogue <u>might</u> say, "They think I'm incompetent."
        - **Feeling**: A tightness forms in your chest, maybe your stomach knots up.
    - Because you've had past experiences of feeling unappreciated, you assign a meaning of "I'm being judged or blamed."
    - This then triggers a sense of defensiveness. Maybe you shut down, tense up, or start planning a snippy comeback.
3. **Result**
    - Your emotional state (defensiveness) leads you to either clam up or snap back. Now the rest of the meeting feels like you're under attack, even if no one <u>actually singled you out</u>.
    - This pattern repeats over time, and with different experiences, reinforcing an unresourceful limiting belief like "No one respects me," which can keep you stuck in victim mode.

*Meanwhile, the **reality could be** that your coworker was rolling their eyes at a text they just received, or they're annoyed about an unrelated issue. Your subconscious mind filtered the situation to fit a negative storyline. By becoming aware of these filters and how you create **meaning**, you gain the power to pause, question your interpretation, and choose a more resourceful response.*

Question: As you were reading the example, did you find yourself saying something like, "that's not what that eye roll meant!?" Sweet. You just experienced exactly what you just learned: Everyone has their own filters and assigns their own meaning to things. 😊

Now, what if you realized that every time you shut down in the middle of a disagreement, feel anxious in a meeting, or judge yourself in the mirror, it's not "just the way you are" but a pattern you have the power to change? Suddenly, even the toughest challenges become an invitation to rewrite your mental movie. You'd harness that 5% of your conscious mind and give **new** marching orders to the other 95%. Imagine living in a reality where you choose which beliefs to reinforce and which ones to throw out. Where you're not just reacting to life but actively creating it.

The more you own this Model of Reality, the more you'll realize you've just been running on outdated "software", and the best part is, now you've got the power to upgrade it!

Renegade Reflection:

You are the filmmaker of your own mental movies. So **edit them.** Dismantle any unresourceful old meaning that keeps you avoiding your most empowered, aligned, authentic self. And remember what Wayne Dyer said: *"When you change the way you look at things, the things you look at change."*

When I face conflict, what would happen if I paused and asked: "What's another way to see this?"

_____
_____
_____
_____
_____

In what ways am I <u>deleting</u> evidence of progress or success in my life due to the limiting beliefs I have of myself?

_____
_____
_____
_____
_____

What does my physiology look like when I'm feeling the most empowered, and how can I replicate that right now? *(write this one out, then do it now! Move your body, fix your posture, etc).*

_____
_____
_____
_____
_____

Notes For Integration:

📢 **Let's Stay Connected — Your Breakthroughs Matter!**

I wonder how many ways you can already feel yourself **shifting**? How many moments today will prove that your **transformation is already happening**?

🚀 **Go on a treasure hunt**, every single day, looking for evidence that you're already showing up differently, thinking differently, and seeing the world through a new lens.

And when you find those moments? **I want to hear all about them.**

💥 Your expanded awareness.
💥 Your mindset shifts.
💥 Your holy-shit-I-see-it-now breakthroughs.
💥 Your moments of **pure, undeniable transformation**.

Because this isn't just about reading a book. **This is about becoming.**

📧 **Email me:**
Hello@TheLotusBanks.com

📲 **Tag me on FB & Insta:**
@Lotus.Banks

🔥 Your success is happening in real-time. Let's celebrate it together.

"The number one key to success in life is to master your own state. If you can manage and master your state, there's nothing you can't do."

TONY ROBBINS

Level Six

STATE MANAGEMENT

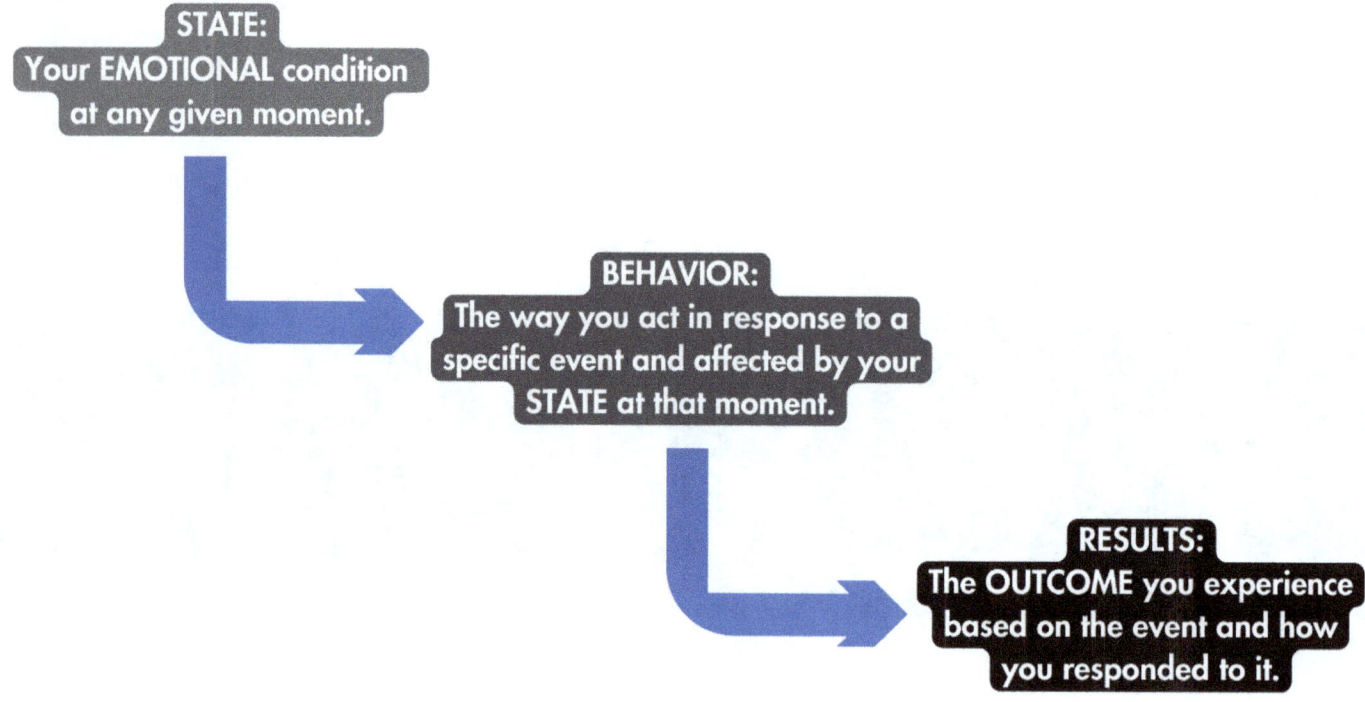

Have you ever felt like you knew exactly what to do next but couldn't make yourself do it? Or maybe you notice you're behaving in ways that sabotage your own progress? That's because your **state** (your emotional condition at any given moment) is the key factor that affects how you behave and ultimately, the results you get in life.

Consider these two equations:
1. E (Event) + S (State) = B (Behavior)
2. E (Event) + B (Behavior) = R (Results)

In other words, any event in your life plus the emotional state you're in affects the behavior you choose in that moment. That behavior then shapes your results. If your state is unresourceful, your behavior will likely follow suit, and you'll keep getting the same old results. The only way to disrupt the loop is to shift your state — because if you change your state, your behavior and results change too.

Upgrade your **state**. Upgrade your **behavior**. Upgrade your **results**.

Your **state** is driven by two main factors:
1. **The Meaning You Give to Your Mental Movies** (Pictures, Sounds, Feelings)
    - This meaning and interpretation is heavily influenced by old programming: learned patterns from childhood, past experiences, and your personal beliefs and values.
2. **Physiology**
    - How you hold and move your body: posture, breath, facial expressions, etc.
    - A slumped posture or shallow breathing can feed negative states, while standing tall or breathing deeply can <u>instantly</u> generate a more resourceful state.

Combine these, and you create an emotional condition (state) that either propels you forward or keeps you stuck.

Consider the cell phone analogy: if you never update your device, it'll eventually glitch and fail. The same goes for your **internal operating system** (the subconscious mind).

Elements to consider and come back to frequently:

Acknowledge the Equations: External Events (E) are always occurring: a tough work deadline, an argument with a loved one, or a sudden opportunity. The moment you add your **state** (S) into the equation, your behavior (B) is affected. Over time, that behavior determines your results (R).

Upgrade Your Physiology: If you're in a slump, stand up, roll your shoulders back, and take a few slow, intentional breaths. The moment your body language shifts, your brain receives new signals, and your emotional state can follow.

Now, imagine if you fully owned your state every single day? You'd see how becoming aware of and shifting your state alters your behavior, and altering your behavior recalibrates your results. That's how you move from feeling stuck to feeling empowered, courageous, and "enough" to handle whatever life is throwing your way. When you realize your state is the backbone in these two equations, the power to transform your life is literally in your hands.

State Snapshots:

Objective: Build awareness of how often your state shifts subconsciously.

Instructions: Set 3 alarms on your phone for different times of the day. Each time one goes off, pause and ask yourself these 4 questions:
1. What's my current state? (Name what and how you're feeling emotionally)
2. How am I holding my body? (Physiology and posture)
3. What story is running in my head right now? (Thoughts)
4. Where and how could I shift (if needed) **to create a more resourceful state? Do it now!**

Record the answers quickly below (no judging, no editing, no filtering – trust what comes up!)

State Snapshot #1:
 1. _____
 2. _____
 3. _____
 4. _____

State Snapshot #2:
 1. _____
 2. _____
 3. _____
 4. _____

State Snapshot #3:
 1. _____
 2. _____
 3. _____
 4. _____

Reflection: At the end of the day, review your snapshots. Notice any patterns or triggers that showed up repeatedly. Then decide one small adjustment you'll make tomorrow (posture, breathing, or internal dialogue) to influence your state even more consciously.

Renegade Reflection:

What's the biggest "event" in my life right now that's triggering an unresourceful state and how can I shift it?

_____
_____
_____
_____
_____

How do I habitually hold my body or breathe when I'm stressed, and what small change could flip that script in an instant?

_____
_____
_____
_____
_____

Who in my life exemplifies great state management, and how can I model their approach?

_____
_____
_____
_____
_____

If I believed 100% that E + S = B and E + B = R, how would that reshape my view of any current struggle?

_____
_____
_____

Notes For Integration:

🔔 **Let's Stay Connected — Your Breakthroughs Matter!**

I wonder how many ways you can already feel yourself **shifting**? How many moments today will prove that your **transformation is already happening**?

🚀 **Go on a treasure hunt**, every single day, looking for evidence that you're already showing up differently, thinking differently, and seeing the world through a new lens.

And when you find those moments? **I want to hear all about them.**

💥 Your expanded awareness.
💥 Your mindset shifts.
💥 Your holy-shit-I-see-it-now breakthroughs.
💥 Your moments of **pure, undeniable transformation**.

Because this isn't just about reading a book. **This is about becoming.**

📩 **Email me:**
Hello@TheLotusBanks.com

📲 **Tag me on FB & Insta:**
@Lotus.Banks

🔥 Your success is happening in real-time. Let's celebrate it together.

"With the right alignment everything you want makes its way into your experience. You are the keeper of your own gate."

ESTHER HICKS

Level Seven

EFFORT TO ENERGY

Have you ever set a goal, followed all the "logical" steps, and still somehow manage to derail yourself? It's not that you lack discipline or intelligence, you're just out of alignment. You see, the conscious mind is the **goal setter**, but your subconscious mind is the **goal getter**. If these two aren't working together, you might just stay in a cycle of wanting something consciously but sabotaging it subconsciously. And here's the kicker: your subconscious mind is a powerhouse influenced by beliefs, values, memories, past experiences, and filters. It runs the show beneath the surface, just like the part of an iceberg we never see. Without the subconscious on board, all the conscious "effort" in the world might not cut it, because your **energy** isn't aligned with your actions.

Think of your mind like an iceberg (diagram on next page). The top, visible portion above the waterline is your **conscious mind**: the place of logic, planning, and thinking. It's small but loud, telling you exactly what goals you want, or logically <u>should</u> want. Beneath the surface lurks the **subconscious mind**: the endless space that stores beliefs, values, memories, past experiences, and filters. This is where the real magic (or sabotage) happens, because it's in charge of your identity, your sense of possibility, and the energy you bring to every goal you set.

Goal **Setter** vs. Goal **Getter**
- Your **conscious** mind **sets** the targets.
- Your **subconscious** mind determines whether you **actually hit** those targets.

Effort to **Energy**
- **Effort** is conscious: It's the action, the doing, the "checklist" mentality.
- **Energy** is subconscious: It's your emotional drive, your sense of identity, your deeper motivation.

When these two align, when your conscious effort and your subconscious energy pull you in the same direction, you become unstoppable. Without that alignment, you might just keep spinning your wheels, wondering why your goals never quite materialize how you desire.

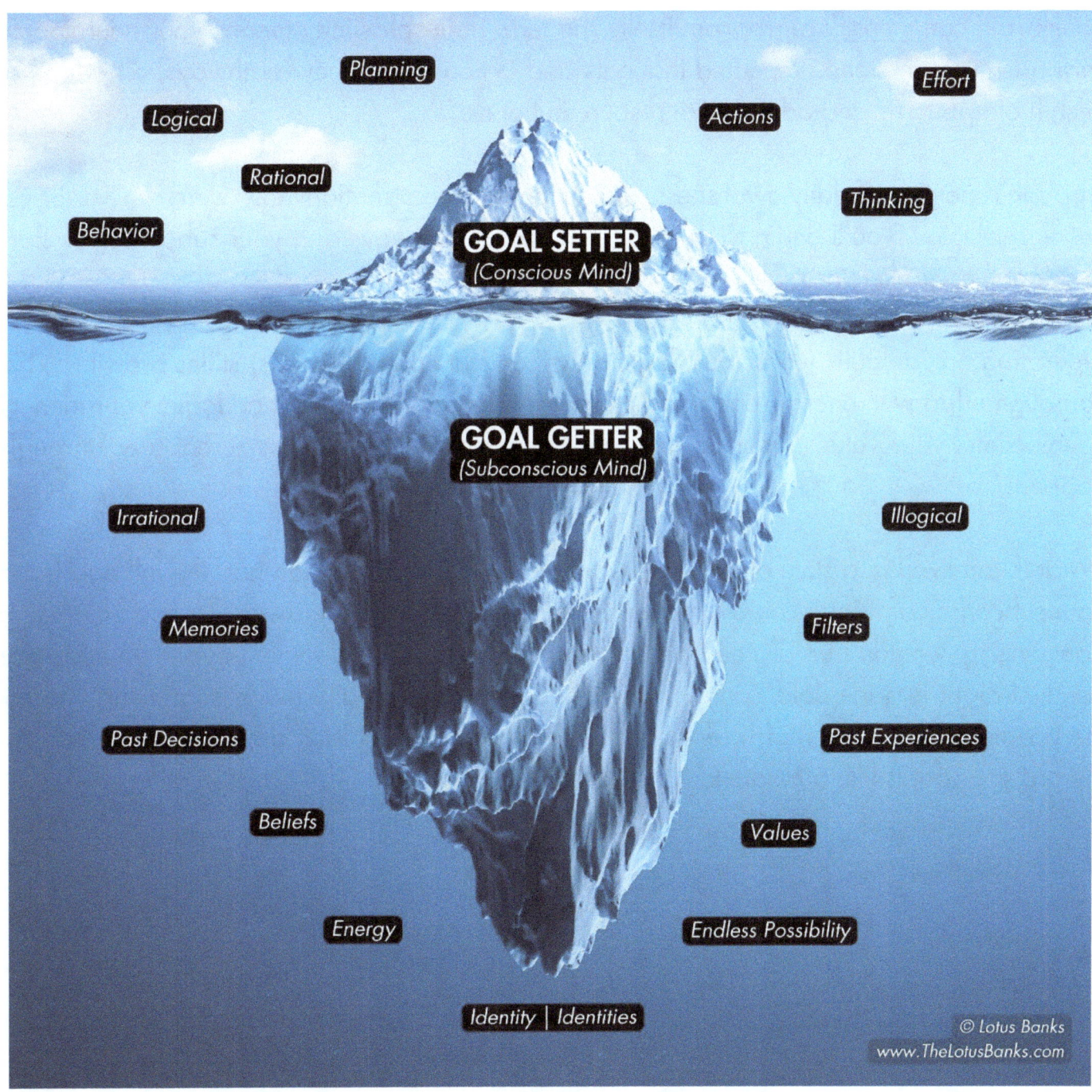

So how do we create alignment, and how is this even possible? I mean our brain is hardwired… right?!?

🔥 **Neuroplasticity has entered the chat.** 🔥

Your brain can <u>literally</u> **reprogram** itself. The term **neuroplasticity** means your neurological wiring isn't set in stone. Repeated thoughts and actions **carve** new pathways, allowing you to shift old patterns and adopt more resourceful ones.

Through repetition of daily awareness, disruption, and reformation (don't worry, we'll dive deep on this a bit later), you'll begin to solidify fresh neural pathways and your subconscious starts to adopt these beliefs as reality.

Operating on "default" (conscious, logic only, comfort zone decisions) stifles growth. When you align effort with energy, engaging the part of you that's **bigger** than logic: your identity, your beliefs, your values, your desires, and your inherent worthiness — real breakthroughs happen!

What if you lived in a state of synergy, where every conscious action had the full backing of your subconscious mind? You'd experience goals manifesting faster, with less internal friction. Your energy wouldn't be drained by battling old doubts. You'd move beyond your comfort zone, straight into the Bold Zone — living, executing, and creating with alignment. Imagine the power, and the relief, of having your entire iceberg (both seen and unseen) pulling you toward your goals like a magnet.

UNLEASH YOUR INNER RENEGADE

Iceberg Inventory:

Objective: Identify subconscious beliefs that might oppose your conscious goals.

Instructions: Using the blank iceberg below. Above the waterline, write down a current goal. Below the water, brain dump every underlying belief, fear, or story of a past experience that might **secretly** sabotage your results.

Take Notice: Which below-the-surface beliefs need rewriting for your subconscious mind to become a true **goal getter**?

Renegade Reflection:

You're the gatekeeper of your own alignment. When you marry **Effort** (conscious doing) with **Energy** (subconscious being), you unlock a force that can move mountains. Keep pushing beyond your comfort zone, keep checking beneath the surface, and watch how quickly your reality begins to transform.

In what ways do I talk myself out of dreaming bigger because it doesn't "make sense" logically?

_____
_____
_____
_____
_____

In which area of my life am I pushing with sheer effort while ignoring my deeper emotional alignment (or lack thereof), and how is this affecting my results?

_____
_____
_____
_____
_____

What subconscious beliefs about myself might be sabotaging the goals my conscious mind sets?

_____
_____
_____
_____
_____

📣 **Let's Stay Connected — Your Breakthroughs Matter!**

I wonder how many ways you can already feel yourself **shifting**? How many moments today will prove that your **transformation is already happening**?

🚀 **Go on a treasure hunt**, every single day, looking for evidence that you're already showing up differently, thinking differently, and seeing the world through a new lens.

And when you find those moments? **I want to hear all about them.**

💥 Your expanded awareness.
💥 Your mindset shifts.
💥 Your holy-shit-I-see-it-now breakthroughs.
💥 Your moments of **pure, undeniable transformation.**

Because this isn't just about reading a book. **This is about becoming.**

📩 **Email me:**
Hello@TheLotusBanks.com

📲 **Tag me on FB & Insta:**
@Lotus.Banks

🔥 Your success is happening in real-time. Let's celebrate it together.

"Whatever you believe, your cells believe too. They don't question anything. They hear every thought, feeling, and belief you have."

RHONDA BYRNE

UNLEASH YOUR INNER RENEGADE

Level Eight

FORM OF INTELLIGENCE

Have you ever had a thought so stressful that it gave you a headache, or a moment of excitement so intense you felt a rush of energy pulse through your entire body? That's no coincidence. Every thought you have releases neurochemical messengers, often called "thought chemicals", that travel throughout your body, influencing not only your emotions but your physical state as well. Your cells are constantly eavesdropping on your internal dialogue. When you focus on a particular thought, you quite literally **feel** it in every cell of your body.

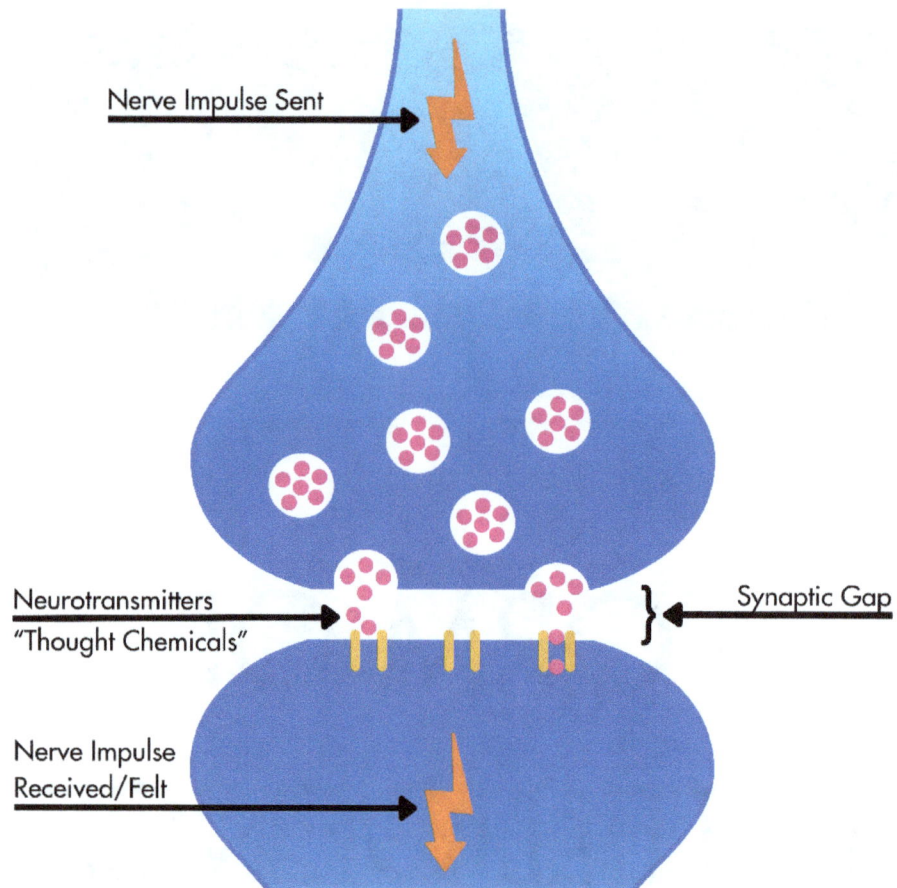

Why does this matter? Because if you want to create lasting change, you must understand that your mind isn't just in your head; it's an entire mind-body system. When you shift your thinking, you shift the messages your cells receive, affecting your energy, health, and overall sense of well-being.

Neurotransmitters, or "thought chemicals", are the messengers that carry signals from one neuron to another, enabling communication throughout your entire nervous system. Think of them as a cosmic game of telephone, except instead of passing rumors, they pass along your beliefs, emotions, and intentions.

Here's how it works:

1. **Brain Fires a Thought**: You think about something (a goal, a memory, a limiting belief), which triggers electrical impulses in the brain.
2. **Neurotransmitter Release**: These impulses stimulate the release of neurotransmitters; chemicals like dopamine, serotonin, adrenaline, etc, into the synaptic gap between neurons.
3. **Spreading the Word**: The receiving neuron picks up these signals and relays the message onward. Eventually, these thought chemicals affect cells throughout your entire body, influencing everything from your heartbeat to your immune response.
4. **Beliefs in Every Cell**: Because your cells **don't question** the data they receive, they adopt your thoughts, feelings, and beliefs as *fact!* Whether you believe you're unstoppable or unworthy, your body acts accordingly to prove that what you're thinking is true!

Quick Hitting Tips to Master the Mind/Body Connection:

Own Your Focus: What you focus on, you feel. That means when you obsess over worst-case scenarios, you flood your body with stress chemicals like cortisol and adrenaline. Shift to focusing on solutions, gratitude, or excitement, and you release endorphins and dopamine that fuel motivation and momentum.

Harness Your State: Move your body in ways that welcome positive change. Stand tall, breathe deeply, and visualize your cells lighting up with empowering neurotransmitters. This not only alters your emotional state, it also primes your physiology to accept growth.

Use Visualization & Self-Talk: When you paint a vivid mental picture of success or speak kindly to yourself, you're physically altering the chemistry in your body. Imagine each cell smiling, resonating with your chosen story. This is more than a feel-good trick, it's a biological reality.

Reinforce, Repeat, Rewire: Neuroplasticity (from the previous level) **works hand in hand with** your "thought chemicals." Repetition plus emotion rewires your brain's default settings, transforming fleeting moments of positivity into a sustained baseline.

What if you realized that every single cell in your body is waiting for your next instruction? You're not just a passenger in this life, you're the operator of a biochemical orchestra. Imagine tapping into that power daily — shifting your focus to what you *truly* want and watching your entire system align to make it happen. And the more you do it, the more natural it becomes to feel energized, confident, and ready for whatever life throws at you.

Take Notice:

Objective: Strengthen the mind-body connection using imagery.

Instructions:

1. Take 30 seconds and check in with your current physical and emotional state. Use 5-7 words to describe what you are thinking and what you are feeling in your body.

I am currently thinking/feeling in my body:
_____
_____

2. Now, for the next 3-5 minutes, close your eyes, and vividly imagine each neuron (each cell) firing off tiny bursts of light (neurotransmitters) that ripple through your body. Visualize these sparks spreading love, positivity, healing, or motivation to every cell. While doing so <u>shift</u> your thoughts, your breathing, and how you're holding your body to **align** with the intention you are visualizing.

Reflection: After the visualization, reflect on the positive shift in your emotional and physical state. Compare it to how you felt before you started.

After the visualization I am now feeling/thinking:
_____
_____
_____
_____

Renegade Reflection:

Remember, your body is listening. Each thought, feeling, and belief becomes a chemical conversation with your cells. Choose wisely what you broadcast and watch how quickly your life evolves when every part of you is on board.

What kind of signals am I sending to my body when I talk down to myself or obsess over worst-case scenarios?

_____
_____
_____
_____

How can I leverage the "what you focus on, you feel" principle to steer my day in a more empowered direction?

_____
_____
_____
_____
_____
_____

If I fully believed my cells are eagerly awaiting my next cue, how would I choose to speak, think, and move differently from this moment on?

_____
_____
_____
_____
_____
_____

"The first step to healing is to connect our minds back to our bodies."

STEVEN JAGGERS

Level Nine

BREATHE

Have you ever felt like your emotions were spinning out of control, your thoughts racing a mile a minute, and your body tensing up as if bracing for an invisible punch? These signals are likely **nervous system dysregulation**, a sign your body's trying to protect you from a perceived threat, even if one doesn't truly exist. In a world that moves at breakneck speed, it's easy to forget how radically we can recalibrate by simply returning to our breath.

Breathwork allows you to surrender to the moment and move through everything that is not real while simultaneously reconnecting yourself to all that you are.

In other words, the breath isn't just for survival. It's a gateway to wholeness — mind, body, and spirit. Whether you're <u>pushing</u> for a goal, <u>pulling</u> in what you desire, or <u>pausing</u> to integrate your growth, your breath is the constant thread that keeps your mind and body aligned.

Original Responses vs. Unresourceful Patterns

Once upon a time, your body's intense reaction to stress or a situation was actually intelligent. It served as a protective mechanism, shutting down unnecessary processes, pumping adrenaline, and focusing on pure survival. This was **resourceful.** However, somewhere along the way, that originally adaptive (resourceful) response can become maladaptive (**unresourceful**). The body then stays stuck in a high-alert mode, even when there's no real threat present. Old emotional or physical reactions settle in as unresourceful "defaults," which can manifest as chronic tension, repressed and suppressed emotions, and even illness (what I like to refer to as **dis-ease**).

Nervous System Regulation + The Vagus Nerve

- The vagus nerve is like your body's built-in "chill out" system. It acts like the main highway of the parasympathetic nervous system. It helps you "rest and digest" when life isn't throwing you into fight-or-flight.
- Deep, intentional breathing stimulates the vagus nerve, sending calming signals throughout your body and mind. This can help shift you from a state of panic or overdrive to one of calm and focus.
- Properly regulated, you're free to feel, process, and release old stuck emotions rather than constantly living in survival mode.

Push, Pull, Pause
- **Push**: to step beyond your comfort zone when growth calls.
- **Pull**: to focus on magnetizing your desires, aligning your energy and effort – drawing in what you seek.
- **Pause**: to take the time to slow down, integrate, and embody your progress.

Your breath is the **universal remote** for all three phases — fueling your **push**, amplifying your **pull**, and grounding you in your **pause**. By using your breath intentionally, you release unresourceful patterns, letting your body reset and heal.

Quick Hitting Tips to Master Your State Through Your Breath:

- **Vagus Nerve Activation:**
  <u>Longer Exhales</u>: Try inhaling for 3 seconds, exhaling for 6. Longer exhales stimulate the vagus nerve more effectively.
  <u>Humming</u>: Low-frequency sounds (like chanting "OM" or humming) can also activate the vagus nerve, calming your entire nervous system.
- **Somatic Release:** Let your body **move** with the breath. If you feel tension in your chest or body, roll your shoulders, shake your body out, or stretch your arms overhead as you exhale. This helps release trapped energy from your muscles and body.
- **Acknowledge + Let Go:** Remind yourself that your old defensive triggers were once helpful. Thank them for serving you. Then gently guide your body and mind toward a new, more resourceful way of being.
- **Daily Breathwork Practice:** Even 5–10 minutes of guided breathwork each day can rewire your stress response. Over time, your system learns that it's safe to feel and release, rather than hold-on to pain.

Imagine having a built-in "reset button" whenever tension or unresolved emotion resurfaces. One that not only soothes your mind but literally rewires your entire body's reaction to stress. If you harness your breath in this way, triggers become opportunities to heal rather than reasons to shut down. You'll begin opening space for an expansive, more fulfilling future, one where you're no longer chained to outdated unresourceful responses but living as the bold, willing, and seeking renegade you truly are.

Acknowledge + Let Go:

Objective: Honor your old unresourceful responses while freeing yourself to move on.

Instructions: Write a short letter below to a trigger or habit you once needed for survival. Thank it for protecting you, then state your intention to let it go.
- Then, complete 10 rounds of intentional slow, deep breathing.
    - Say to yourself with each inhale: "Thank you. I love you."
    - Say to yourself with each exhale: "I release you. Goodbye."

Write your gratitude and release letter:

_____
_____
_____
_____
_____
_____
_____
_____
_____
_____
_____

Reflection: Observe the emotional relief and sense of closure after the rounds of breathing and journal your thoughts and feelings below.

_____
_____
_____
_____
_____
_____
_____

Renegade Reflection:

Breathing is living, but <u>intentional</u> breathing is transformative. By owning your breath, you reclaim control of your body, your emotions, and ultimately, your future. Let the old triggers go. Inhale your future self. Exhale anything that no longer serves.

When I feel triggered, ask myself, how can I view this as an opportunity to rewrite an outdated script? And then what can I do to master my state in the moment once I have this awareness?

_____
_____
_____
_____

Where in my daily life do I most often catch myself spiraling into dysregulation, and how might breathwork offer a quick reset?

_____
_____
_____
_____
_____
_____

Which triggers were once vital to my survival but now undermine my well-being, and why am I ready to release them?

_____
_____
_____
_____
_____
_____

UNLEASH YOUR INNER RENEGADE

> "Whether you think you **can**, or you think you **can't**, you're right."
>
> — HENRY FORD

Level Ten

RELEASING LIMITING BELIEFS

Do you ever wonder why certain patterns and beliefs keep showing up, no matter what you do? Truth is, a **belief** in its simplest form is just a **decision** — a thought you once had that you just **decided** was true. Wait, wait, wait! Let's run that back one more time. A belief in its simplest form is just a decision — a thought you randomly had one day that you just decided was true! Maybe it protected you, gave you a sense of stability, or was simply modeled to you during childhood. Over time, you gathered "evidence" to reinforce it, morphing a random idea into an ingrained identity. But here's the kicker: if you decided it once, you can **decide** something else **now**. Clinging to old, unresourceful beliefs only keep you stuck. Let's ditch the outdated logic, upgrade your internal software, and step into the future self you've been waiting to become.

Limiting Beliefs are thoughts or decisions that cap your potential. They often start as a form of self-protection, born from fear or an old outdated sense of safety.

Examples:
- "I'm not good with money."
- "I can't trust anyone in relationships."
- "People like me don't succeed at that level."

These beliefs might have seemed resourceful at one point, like maybe they kept you from risk or heartbreak. But the more you repeat them, the more they shape your identity and reality. **Resourceful** beliefs propel you forward; **unresourceful** ones keep you locked in a loop of missed opportunities.

Reframing to Resourcefulness
- Ask: "What could I learn from this belief that would set me free?"
- Acknowledge that the belief once served a purpose—thank it, then let it go.
- Replace it with a new, empowering decision that aligns with who you're becoming.

What if that "random thought" you once decided was a "truth" is actually **just a bullshit story you've been telling yourself**? Imagine the freedom of realizing you can rewrite the script anytime. You stop labeling yourself as "lazy," "unlucky," or "not enough" and start living in the self-image that matches your ambitions. No more waiting for permission. No more carrying stale beliefs that belong in the past. Instead, you choose to embody the powerful renegade who says, "I'm done with this old pattern and I'm creating something better!"

Timeline Shift:

Objective: Find the root cause of a limiting decision and shift into an empowering belief.

Instructions:

1. State your limiting belief/decision:

   _____

2. Ask yourself, when did I decide that? (trust your gut, whatever comes up, go with it!)

3. On the horizontal timeline of your life below, mark the first time you recall this limiting belief, then mark key moments throughout your life that it was reinforced and got stronger.

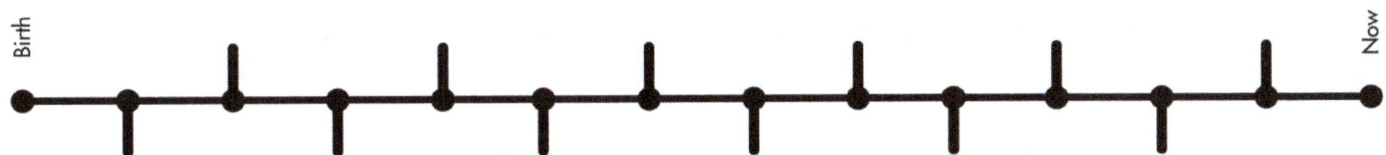

4. Ask yourself, "What do I need to learn from these events, the learnings which will allow me to release this old unresourceful belief easily and effortlessly?
   Write the answers below. Trust your subconscious response. No editing, no filtering. What do you need to LEARN so you can LET GO easily and effortlessly…

   _____

   _____

5. Ask yourself, "Where could I place a new decision, a new empowering belief on this timeline that changes the entire trajectory?" <u>Mark it in a different color or symbol!</u>

6. What are you choosing to believe instead? Write out your new empowering belief.

   _____

   _____

7. Close your eyes and picture yourself six months or a year from now, living fully aligned with your new belief. **Embody it.** Note your posture, facial expressions, how you speak.

8. Each day, find at least one piece of evidence that your new belief holds true…(Example: a small financial win if you're changing money beliefs, or a moment of trust in a relationship).

Renegade Reflection:

The stories we tell ourselves become the realities we live in. You wrote the old script; you can write a new one. Dismantle the beliefs that no longer serve you, and watch your entire world open up with possibility.

What's 1 limiting story about myself I've believed for years, and how has it shaped my results?
_____
_____
_____

What new decision can I make right now that aligns with where I'm headed, not where I've been? (new empowering belief)
_____
_____

In what ways might my relationships, finances, or personal happiness improve if I choose a more empowering narrative?
_____
_____
_____

When the old belief resurfaces, how will I catch and redirect it towards my new perspective?
_____
_____
_____

Who or what around me might reinforce the new belief, and how can I seek more of that influence?
_____
_____

Notes For Integration:

Notes For Integration:

🔔 **Let's Stay Connected — Your Breakthroughs Matter!**

I wonder how many ways you can already feel yourself **shifting**? How many moments today will prove that your **transformation is already happening?**

🚀 **Go on a treasure hunt**, every single day, looking for evidence that you're already showing up differently, thinking differently, and seeing the world through a new lens.

And when you find those moments? **I want to hear all about them.**

💥 Your expanded awareness.
💥 Your mindset shifts.
💥 Your holy-shit-I-see-it-now breakthroughs.
💥 Your moments of **pure, undeniable transformation.**

Because this isn't just about reading a book. **This is about becoming.**

📩 **Email me:**
Hello@TheLotusBanks.com

📱 **Tag me on FB & Insta:**
@Lotus.Banks

🔥 **Your success is happening in real-time. Let's celebrate it together.**

***There are also extra pages at the end of this book for you to continue to flip the script on any additional old, outdated, limiting beliefs/decisions; transforming them into new, empowering resourceful beliefs.

> "If all you see is what you see, you do not see all there is to be seen."

MIKE SIGNORELLI

Level Eleven

FOUR GEARS TO INITIATE PROGRESS™

Do you ever feel like you're spinning your wheels, taking small actions here and there but never truly breaking through? The truth is: **change** will happen whether you want it to or not, life is always shifting. But **progress** is a choice. Progress demands you become aware, make a firm decision, upgrade your beliefs, and then take aligned action. That's what these Four Gears are all about – tapping into your personal power to create real, lasting results.

Think about it: the day you decide to be honest with yourself, take ownership of your situation, and do whatever it takes to move forward – **that's** the day you start steering your own life. You're no longer a passenger. You are the driver, calibrating your direction and pace.

Four Gears To Initiate Progress™

Four Gears to Initiate Progress™ are interconnected steps that turn potential into reality:

1. **Awareness**
    - You can't change what you're not willing to see. Awareness is about confronting the truth of your situation, no matter how uncomfortable.
    - <u>Key Question</u>: "What am I pretending not to know?"
2. **Decision**
    - <u>Decision</u> literally means "to cut off" any other possibility. When you decide, you shift from "maybe" to "must."
    - <u>Key Question</u>: "What **must** change now that I know this?"

3. **Belief**
    - Your subconscious mind carries beliefs from old experiences, some resourceful, some not. The moment you form a new belief, you open the door to new behaviors.
    - <u>Key Question</u>: "What would I have to **believe** about myself to make this change?"
4. **Action**
    - Awareness + Decision + Belief won't matter if you don't take action.
    - <u>Key Question</u>: "What's the first **micro** step I will now take to make this change?"

When all four gears engage, you create forward motion. Progress.

If one gear is stuck: say, you might have awareness, but you never decide to do anything about it — you stay in place, stuck in potential without ever experiencing the reality you desire.

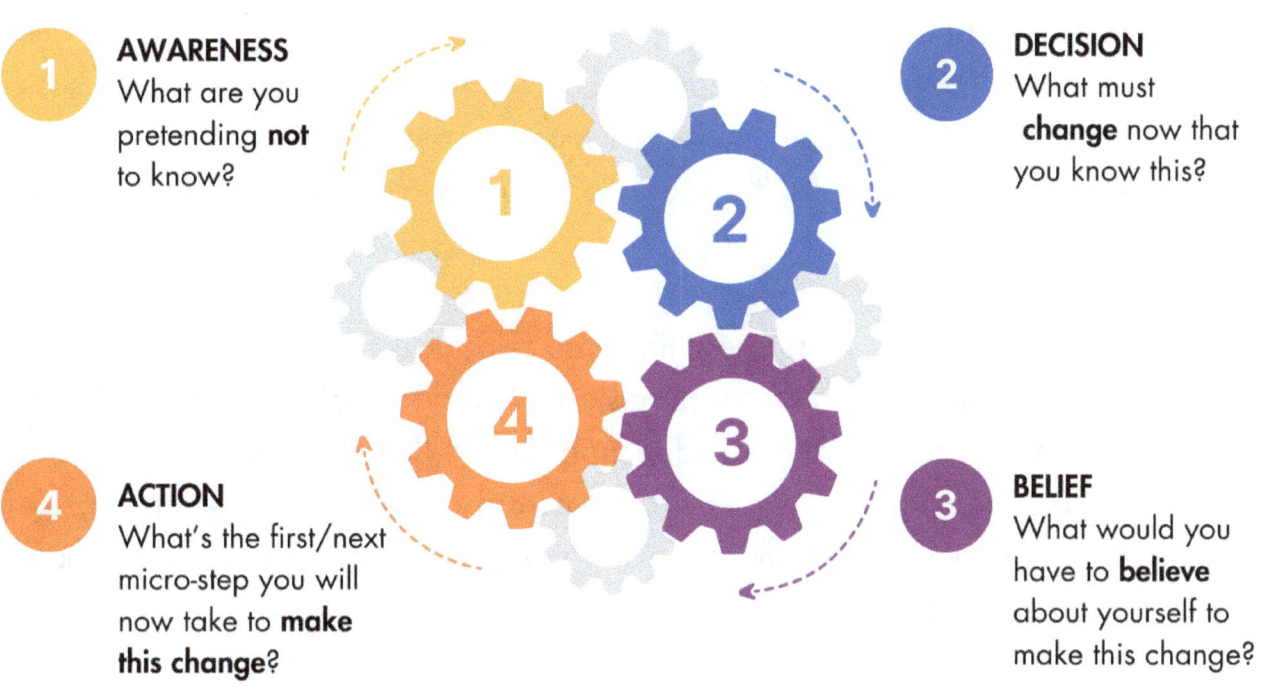

In a moment, you're going to dive in **deep** and put these gears to work. Here's the no-bullshit approach to get the biggest transformation and shift from this process.

Engage Gear 1: Awareness
- Take a brutally honest look at your life.
- Ask: "What am I **pretending not** to know?"
- Maybe it's that your job is draining your soul, or your unhealthy habits are stalling your dreams. Shine a light on it.

Engage Gear 2: Decision
- Once you see the truth, you have a choice: **keep lying to yourself or shift.**
- Stand in front of a mirror and say out loud, "I'm done tolerating this."
- **Decide now.** Ask, "What **must change** now that I know this?"

Engage Gear 3: Belief
- Ask yourself, "What would I have to **believe** about myself to make this change?
- If you've been telling yourself, "I'm unworthy," flip it into "I am more than enough for the life I desire."
- Breathe into that new statement, let it settle. Embody it.

Engage Gear 4: Action
- Start small. Maybe you research a course, make that phone call, or toss out the junk food. Tiny moves now are better than massive moves **never**.
- **Celebrate each shift!** It's proof to your subconscious you're no longer just talking.

Imagine you used these Four Gears every time you felt stuck. First, you'd face the unfiltered reality (Awareness). Then you'd commit (Decision)! No more half-in, half-out. Next, you'd upgrade your beliefs to match your new direction (Belief). Finally, you'd back it all up with consistent, tangible micro-steps (Action). You'd create unstoppable momentum, fueling a journey toward being more, doing more, having more, and giving more. That's the essence of progress: stepping boldly into who you're meant to be.

Gear Initiation:

Objective: Cultivate deeper awareness and self-honesty.

Engage Gear 1 (Awareness): Take a brutally honest look at your life.

Ask yourself: "What am I **pretending not** to know?" Then brain dump everything that comes up. Trust your subconscious mind. No filtering. No editing. Trust what comes up. Go!

_____
_____
_____
_____
_____

Once you see the truth, you have a choice: **keep lying to yourself or shift.** Stand in front of a mirror and say out loud, "I am done tolerating this."

Engage Gear 2 (Decision): Once you see the truth, you have a choice: **keep lying to yourself or shift. Decide now.**

Ask yourself, "What **must change** now that I know this?" You know the deal. Trust your subconscious mind. No filtering. No editing. Go!

_____
_____
_____
_____
_____

Engage Gear 3 (Belief): If you've been telling yourself, "I'm unworthy," or any other bullshit limiting belief – the time is **now** to flip the script! What's on the other side of that limiting belief? The more empowering belief!

Ask yourself, "What would I have to **believe** about myself to make this change?

_____
_____
_____
_____
_____

Breathe it in! This is you. This has always been you. Let it settle. Embody it.

Engage Gear 4 (Action): Start small. Show your subconscious mind the rewiring and reprogramming starts right now!

Ask yourself, "What's the first few micro-steps I will take **now** to **make this change?**

_____
_____
_____
_____
_____

Now celebrate! It's proof to your subconscious you're no longer just talking. You're putting this in motion! Your next level starts now!

Renegade Reflection:

The only thing standing between you and your next level is a **willingness** to see what you're avoiding, **decide** it's time to change, **believe** you can do it, and **take the action** that proves you mean it. Remember: you're not after mere change. You're after progress. So, rev up those Four Gears and start creating the life you know you deserve.

What's one current challenge I've been pretending not to see clearly, and how might confronting it change my life?

_____
_____
_____
_____
_____

In what ways do I fool myself into thinking I've 'decided,' when really, I'm still sitting on the fence?

_____
_____
_____
_____
_____

How could a single new belief about my worthiness or capability unlock more progress for me right now?

_____
_____
_____
_____
_____

What micro step can I take today to prove I'm not just talking, but truly taking action?
_____
_____
_____
_____
_____

With these Four Gears, how will my life look in six months if I consistently engage each one?
_____
_____
_____
_____
_____

📣 Let's Stay Connected — Your Breakthroughs Matter!

I wonder how many ways you can already feel yourself **shifting**? How many moments today will prove that your **transformation is already happening**?

🚀 **Go on a treasure hunt**, every single day, looking for evidence that you're already showing up differently, thinking differently, and seeing the world through a new lens.

And when you find those moments? **I want to hear all about them.**

💥 Your expanded awareness.
💥 Your mindset shifts.
💥 Your holy-shit-I-see-it-now breakthroughs.
💥 Your moments of **pure, undeniable transformation.**

📧 **Email me:**
Hello@TheLotusBanks.com

📱 **Tag me on FB & Insta:**
@Lotus.Banks

🔥 Your success is happening in real-time. Let's celebrate it together.

Notes For Integration:

"Whatever we plant in our subconscious mind and nourish with repetition and emotion will one day become a reality."

EARL NIGHTINGALE

UNLEASH YOUR INNER RENEGADE

Level Twelve

PADRR™

We've explored how your subconscious mind drives 95% of your actions, forming patterns and strategies for everything you do. But what happens when these patterns stop serving you? You can't simply *wish* them away. You must rewrite the code that's running the show. Enter **PADRR**™, a four-step process designed to **retrain and rewire** your brain. By systematically **becoming aware**, **disrupting**, **reforming**, and **repeating** new, resourceful patterns, you transform not just a single behavior but your entire reality. Every day becomes an upgrade, moving you closer to the future self you're ready to embody.

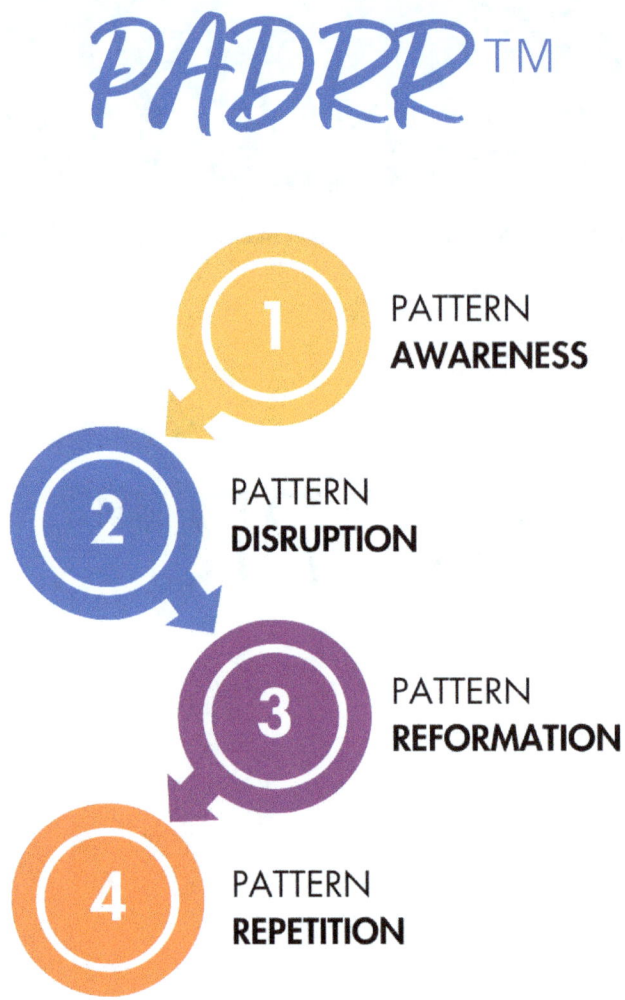

Think of it like **updating your internal software**. Instead of letting outdated, unresourceful strategies and patterns run the show, you're now the programmer, writing new, aligned code that supports your growth and your goals.

Pattern Awareness
You can't change what you pretend not to see. Often, we know a pattern exists, like procrastinating on important tasks, snapping at loved ones under stress, or emotional eating – but we hide from the truth to avoid discomfort. (Ouch!) Step one is shining a light on it. The moment you acknowledge a pattern is the moment you start to disarm its hold on you.

Pattern Disruption
Once you catch yourself mid-pattern, **disrupt** it on the spot! That means **stop the old behavior right there!** In order to do this, you must create a disruption cue that will instantaneously shift your focus. This abrupt interference tells your brain, "We're not doing this anymore."

Pattern Reformation
Disruption alone won't stick unless you replace the old habit with a **new, resourceful** one. Identify what would serve your future self – a calmer response, a more productive approach, a healthier coping mechanism – and **do that instead**. Your mind might freak out because it's unfamiliar. That's normal. Push past the Dread Zone, step into the Bold Zone, and try on the new behavior. Remember: it's only "weird" because it's new and there's only resistance because your brain doesn't understand this new response (yet).

Pattern Repetition
You can't carve a new neural pathway overnight. Repetition cements the new pattern, so your subconscious eventually defaults to it automatically. Each time the old pattern tries to sneak in, disrupt it again, and reapply your new behavior. Over time, your brain learns, "Ah, this is how we do this now," and upgrades your default setting.

Here's some examples of what this process could look like:

1. **Pattern Awareness**
   - Identify Your Target Pattern. Pick one unresourceful pattern you're ready to change, maybe it's negative self-talk or checking out and shutting down when stressed. Make it your mission to become hyper-alert whenever it arises.

2. **Pattern Disruption**
   - Create a Disruption Cue. Keep it simple: a word, phrase, or physical action (like snapping your fingers or literally saying "stop"). The second you notice the pattern starting, trigger that cue to break the cycle and shift your focus.

3. **Pattern Reformation**
   - Decide on the Replacement Behavior. If your old pattern is, say, scrolling social media, your new pattern could be a 5-minute walk or journaling a quick to-do list. If you lash out in anger, your replacement might be a 3-breath pause followed by asking a clarifying question. Have the replacement **ready**, so you don't freeze when the moment comes.

4. **Pattern Repetition.**
   - Rinse and repeat. Every time the old pattern surfaces, disrupt it in the moment and choose the new behavior/action. Over time, you'll see the shift from forced effort to an effortless habit.

5. **Grace.**
   - This is an "unofficial" step in the process, **yet**, is incredibly important. You've never done this before. You've never worked your brain in this way before. It's bound to be messy in the beginning and maybe even at times throughout the process. Give yourself grace. You're learning. You're making new choices. Love yourself in these moments. It is evidence of your growth, simply by choosing a new action.

Note: You may not have success the first time. Try different disruption cue's and different more resourceful actions until you find the one that works for you (and for this pattern in particular).

What if every limiting pattern in your life could be systematically upgraded, just by *practicing pattern awareness, disruption, reformation, and repetition*? You'd no longer feel controlled by old habits. You'd actively shape your mind. Over time, you'd see a cascade of transformations: healthier relationships, improved finances, more confidence, and a deeper sense of self-alignment. And the best part? **You** are the one making it happen, one pattern at a time.

Intentional Disruption:

PART ONE: PATTERN LOG

Objective: Pinpoint your most unresourceful patterns.

Instructions: For the next 24 hours, note each time you catch yourself in an unresourceful pattern. Write down the trigger, and the immediate thoughts or actions you took. (Part One is time for awareness ONLY. No disruption, yet.)

<u>Triggered Old Unresourceful Pattern:</u>
It may be helpful to use this structure, or something similar to write it out:

I noticed that when (trigger / event/ situation) happens,
I respond in/with (the action, behavior or vocal response you use).
This is unresourceful, because I want to create (what you want to experience instead).

Example:
I noticed that when my partner asks me what I'm doing today, I respond with defensiveness because I made up that they think I'm lazy. This is unresourceful, because I want to create a loving, vulnerable, connected relationship instead.

Now, it's your turn.
Pay attention to your unresourceful patterns over the next 24 hours. <u>Write each one down.</u>

Triggered Old Unresourceful Pattern:
_____
_____
_____
_____

Triggered Old Unresourceful Pattern:
_____
_____
_____
_____

Triggered Old Unresourceful Pattern:
_____
_____
_____
_____

Triggered Old Unresourceful Pattern:
_____
_____
_____
_____

Triggered Old Unresourceful Pattern:
_____
_____
_____
_____

Triggered Old Unresourceful Pattern:
_____
_____
_____
_____

Triggered Old Unresourceful Pattern:
_____
_____
_____
_____

Triggered Old Unresourceful Pattern:
_____
_____
_____
_____

Intentional Disruption:

PART TWO: INTERRUPT + SWAP

Objective: Get comfortable with disrupting a habit in real time.

Instructions:
1. Choose one pattern to focus on from Part One.
2. Create a Disruption Cue: Keep it simple: a word, phrase, or physical action (like snapping your fingers or literally saying "stop").
3. Decide what you do instead of the old pattern/behavior/habit. A more resourceful choice.

If your cue and your new resourceful action work, then continue to step 4. If not, try another/new/different cue or action until you find the strategy that works. Then continue to step 4.

4. Rinse and repeat.

Example:

Old, triggered, unresourceful pattern:
I noticed that when my partner asks me what I'm doing today, I respond with defensiveness because I made up that they think I'm lazy. This is unresourceful, because I want to create a loving, vulnerable, connected relationship instead.

Interrupt + Swap:
When my partner asks me what I'm doing today, instead of getting defensive, I will pause and take a slow and intentional inhale and exhale. Then I will respond with what my plans are from a loving and connected place.

Tip: The stronger the **emotional charge** you have in the moment of your unresourceful pattern, the more 'disruptive' the pattern interrupt cue needs to be. I've used many before. Some **examples of those I've personally tried:** intentional breathing, 5 second pause before acting, snapping my fingers, screaming in a pillow, running a lap around my house, doing 5 jumping jack or air squats, asking for space and committing to a time to come back to the conversation, clapping my hands, patting myself on the shoulder, jumping up and down, etc. **It doesn't matter what you do to interrupt the pattern – just do <u>something</u>** that interrupts your attention in that moment!

UNLEASH YOUR INNER RENEGADE

Intentional Disruption:

PART TWO: INTERRUPT + SWAP
(CONTINUED FROM PREVIOUS PAGE)

Now, it's your turn.
Choose (1) unresourceful pattern from Part One.

Write out your new PADRR™ strategy.

1. **Pattern Awareness:** Write out the unresourceful pattern.
   _____
   _____
   _____
   _____

2. **Pattern Disruption:** Decide on a few options for the cue(s) to test and interrupt the old pattern in the moment. Circle which one works.
   _____
   _____
   _____
   _____

3. **Pattern Reformation:** Decide what you want to do instead. Write down a few options for the new more resourceful pattern/action/response to try. Circle which one works.
   _____
   _____
   _____
   _____

4. **Pattern Repetition:** Once you find a cue and action that works… Rinse and repeat every time the old pattern shows up. You got this!

5. **Grace:** Give yourself love, acceptance and grace in the moment. Allow it to be messy at first and commit to becoming 1% better each time the old pattern resurfaces. Acknowledge to yourself that no matter how messy, this is already evidence of your growth simply because you are choosing a different, more resourceful response.

Renegade Reflection:

Remember, you are the architect of your patterns and strategies. **PADRR**™ is your blueprint for building the mental and emotional framework that supports your growth. When you **see** what's holding you back, **disrupt** it in real time, **reform** it with a bolder, better action, and **repeat** until it sticks, you'll watch your entire life transform, one upgraded pattern at a time.

Which old pattern is costing me the most in terms of energy, relationships, or success, and why am I ready to change it now?

_____
_____
_____
_____

How do I typically dodge awareness by pretending not to see my own behavior?

_____
_____
_____
_____

What motivating anchor (like a personal mantra or vision of my future self) can I tap into whenever I need an extra push?

_____
_____
_____
_____

How will I measure my progress and celebrate small victories as I repeat the new pattern?

_____
_____
_____
_____

If I believed 100% that I can rewire and retrain my brain, what else might become possible for me?

_____
_____
_____
_____

"The only toxic relationship I ever had is the one I had with myself... everyone else was just a reflection of that."

UNKNOWN

Level Thirteen

MIRROR, MIRROR

Have you ever wondered why certain people trigger you like nobody else can? Or why you find yourself admiring qualities in others that you feel you lack? Here's the raw truth: every interaction <u>is a reflection of something</u> **within you**. That friend who gets on your nerves? They're holding up a mirror to the parts of yourself you resist owning. The admired mentor who radiates confidence? You're recognizing a spark that's already waiting inside you. This is the essence of the **universal law of mirrors** – we can't see in others what doesn't also exist in us.

But this isn't about beating yourself up or putting others on a pedestal. It's about claiming responsibility. The flip side of "they're just reflecting what's in me" is, "I have the power to change!" The moment you see that everything you experience, internally and externally, are simply just clues to your own inner world, you step away from blame or envy and into personal growth.

The Mirror Effect

1. **Seeing Our Triggers**
    - If someone's behavior enrages, annoys, or deeply offends you, it's worth asking, "Where in my life do I exhibit a version of that behavior, even if subtle or in different circumstances?"
2. **Seeing Our Admirations**
    - When you find yourself in awe of someone's kindness, creativity, or resilience, that's your subconscious mind recognizing a potential you already have. Otherwise, you wouldn't be able to see and notice it in them.
3. **Choosing Grace and Growth**
    - Instead of rushing to judge or praise, we can choose curiosity.
    - "What is this reflecting back to me about who I am, or who I can be?"
    - If someone is lashing out, remember the words of Thich Nhat Hanh: *"People in deep suffering often spill that suffering onto others. They don't need punishment; they need help."*

When you realize every encounter reveals another piece of you, daily annoyances and inspirations become catalysts for growth. The better you understand your reflection, the better you can create the version of yourself you truly want to see.

So now as you walk through the world, envision everything in it as simply a mirror.

Pause & Reflect
Next time someone triggers you, positive or negative, check your internal mirror.
Ask, "What is this person showing me about myself?"

Unpack the Emotion
If it's anger, is it because you dislike that same tendency in yourself?
If it's admiration, are you yearning to express that trait more openly?

Offer Grace
When faced with unresourceful behavior in others, try responding with gentleness.
That might be exactly what **you** would hope for if you were having a rough day.

Model the World You Want
If you crave more compassion, show it.
If you value honesty, practice it relentlessly.
Be the version of yourself you want to see mirrored back in the world.

Check Your Inner Circle
Look at the three people you spend the most time with.
Which qualities, both inspiring and aggravating, do you see in them, and how might they reflect aspects of you?

What if, instead of reacting to people who drive you nuts, you used that moment to uncover the part of yourself that's craving attention or healing? And imagine if you embraced the qualities you admire in others as a reflection of your own unrealized gifts…how might that boost your confidence, your sense of purpose, and your ability to lead a life aligned with your highest vision?

By understanding the mirror, you take charge of the life you see in front of you each day.

Admiration Inventory:

Objective: Discover your hidden strengths.

Instructions: List three people you admire (they can be friends, family, people you work with, public figures). Next to each person's name, note the qualities you love and respect about them.

Person #1:
_____
_____
_____

Person #2:
_____
_____
_____

Person #3:
_____
_____
_____

Reflection: Now get curious about where these traits already exist within you. Write about what would have to happen for them to show up? And how can you cultivate them more?
_____
_____
_____
_____
_____
_____
_____

Renegade Reflection:

Every person who crosses your path is an opportunity to see more of yourself, the good, the unresourceful, and the potential still waiting to be unleashed. Choose to honor that reflection, and watch how your relationships, and your reality, evolve for the better.

Who's the last person that triggered me, and what might that say about my own hidden patterns or fears?
___
___
___

How often do I blame others for my reactions, rather than investigating and getting curious about what's happening inside me?
___
___
___

What do the three people closest to me reveal about my own qualities, both resourceful and unresourceful?
___
___
___
___

When I admire someone, do I dismiss their traits as unattainable, or do I recognize them as potential within me?
___
___
___

What does showing grace to someone in pain or acting out teach me about the grace I could show myself?
___
___
___

📣 **Let's Stay Connected — Your Breakthroughs Matter!**

I wonder how many ways you can already feel yourself **shifting**? How many moments today will prove that your **transformation is already happening**?

🚀 **Go on a treasure hunt**, every single day, looking for evidence that you're already showing up differently, thinking differently, and seeing the world through a new lens.

And when you find those moments? **I want to hear all about them.**

💥 Your expanded awareness.
💥 Your mindset shifts.
💥 Your holy-shit-I-see-it-now breakthroughs.
💥 Your moments of **pure, undeniable transformation**.

Because this isn't just about reading a book. **This is about becoming.**

📧 **Email me:**
Hello@TheLotusBanks.com

📱 **Tag me on FB & Insta:**
@Lotus.Banks

🔥 Your success is happening in real-time. Let's celebrate it together.

Notes For Integration:

> "A vision is not just a picture of what could be; it is an appeal to better ourselves, a call to become something more."

ROSABETH MOSS KANTER

Level Fourteen

VISUALIZE YOUR FUTURE

After all the digging, releasing, reframing, and rewiring, it's time to bring everything together and focus forward. You didn't do all this work just to stay the same. You're here to *activate* that future self you've been flirting with – the version of you who's braver, bolder, and unapologetically alive. Visualizing your future isn't just daydreaming; it's a call to action. When you see it clearly, feel it deeply, and **know** it's possible, you build a powerful roadmap guiding you toward that reality. Every micro-action you take, every next step, becomes a brick in the foundation of your vision.

Visualizing your future is more than painting a pretty picture. It's about engaging all five senses – sight, sound, touch, taste, smell – to ignite your neurology and imprint your subconscious mind with the outcome you want. By doing so, you're literally rewiring your brain to look for opportunities, solutions, and synchronicities that support your goal.

But, remember: Without action, a vision is just a fantasy. So, here's the formula:

1. **Imagine** your future in sensory-rich detail.
2. **Feel** the emotions of already living that future.
3. **Schedule** small daily micro-steps to make it real.
4. **Know** that the real you exists in the doing, not the wishing.

Quick Hitting Tips to Master Your Visualization:

1. **Set an Achievable Outcome**
   - It's not enough to say "I want a better life." Be specific. Do you want to double your income in six months? Complete a half-marathon? Launch your business? The more specific and measurable, the clearer the path.
2. **Activate All Five Senses**
   - **Sight**: Visualize the environment where you've reached your goal. Colors, surroundings, and even what you might be wearing.
   - **Sound**: What conversations are you having? What does success sound like to you: applause, laughter, the ring of a new client calling?
   - **Touch**: How does it feel physically: relaxed shoulders, energized posture, a handshake that seals the deal?
   - **Taste**: Imagine the celebratory meal, the morning coffee that tastes extra sweet because you *did it.*

- **Smell**: The fresh air of a new place, or the subtle scent that represents victory to you.
3. **Feel It to Seal It**
    - Emotions are the glue that binds vision to reality. Let the feelings of pride, gratitude, and excitement flood your body. When you attach strong emotions, your subconscious mind takes note.
4. **Schedule Micro-Actions**
    - Break down your big vision into daily or weekly steps. If your goal is weight loss, schedule your workout times. If it's a new career, slot in 30 minutes a day to research or refine your skills.
5. **Review & Refine**
    - Keep revisiting your vision. If something shifts – your goals, circumstances, or even your interests, that's okay. Tweak the vision to stay aligned with your evolving self.

What if you approached your future the way a top athlete approaches a gold medal, visualizing the win so vividly that your body and mind believe it's already yours? Each micro-action then feels like an inevitable step, rather than a chore. You'd supercharge your confidence, your resilience, and your motivation. Instead of stumbling forward with uncertainty, you'd walk with purpose, trusting that the future you're shaping is not just some distant dream, but a reality you're actively building – one clear vision and one small step at a time.

Activate Your Future Self

Objective: Activate a higher emotional frequency by aligning with the person you're becoming.

Instructions: Write a letter from your future self who has already mastered these workbook concepts, thanking your present self for the choices you're making, and the progress you have already made.

(continued on next page)

Future Self Letter Template: (review the template, then create your own on the next page)

1. **It is now (enter future date).**
   Enter the date of your future that you are stepping into. Is it a year from now? 6 months? Choose a date within the next 12 months.

2. **Describe in vivid detail what your life looks like as of this date. Include all areas of life from the Circle of Clarity™:** Personal Growth, Professional Growth, Physical Body, Fun + Leisure, Wealth, and Connection

3. **Activate All Five Senses**
   Sight: What do you see in the environment where you've reached your goal. Colors, surroundings, and even what you might be wearing.
   Sound: What conversations are you having? What does success sound like? Applause, laughter, the ring of a new client calling?
   Touch: How does it feel physically? Relaxed shoulders, energized posture, a handshake that seals the deal?
   Taste: Imagine the celebratory meal, the morning coffee that tastes extra sweet because you did it. What tastes are you experiencing as this future version of you?
   Smell: What do you smell? The fresh air of a new place, or the subtle scent that represents victory to you?

4. **Feel It to Seal It**
   Emotions are the glue that binds vision to reality. What feelings and emotions does this version of you experience on a regular basis?

5. **Schedule Micro-Actions**
   After the end of your letter, come up with the first 3 micro-steps you are choosing and putting into action **now** to step into this version of yourself **today**. Then do it!

UNLEASH YOUR INNER RENEGADE

Future Self Letter

It is now _____

Renegade Reflection:

This is your chance to dream bigger, feel deeper, and act bolder. Your future self is calling you into that next level, one fueled by clarity, locked in by belief, and powered by consistent action. You've got all the tools. Now it's time to build the life you see in your mind's eye.

What's the single most compelling vision I have for my future, and how clear is it in my mind right now?
_____
_____
_____

When I picture myself accomplishing this outcome, which emotions flood my body, and how do I want to harness them daily?
_____
_____
_____

How would my relationships, finances, health, and mindset transform if I consistently acted from my future self's perspective?
_____
_____
_____
_____

What daily practices – like journaling, meditation, breathwork, etc, keep me anchored in the vision when life gets hectic?
_____
_____
_____

In six months, a year, or five years from now, how will I look back on this moment and thank myself for having the audacity to dream and do?
_____
_____
_____

📣 **Your Future Self is in Motion – and I'd love to read your letters!**

You just wrote a letter from the **version of you who already has it all**, the one who has stepped into their power, disrupted the bullshit, and claimed their next level.

That version of you is real.

Now, it's time to start **finding proof** that you're already becoming them.

🚀 **Look for the evidence**, every single day. Notice the shifts, the small wins, the moments where you respond differently, think bigger, and move with more intention.

And when you do? **I want to hear about it.**

💥 The first signs that your future self is already showing up.
💥 The breakthroughs that made you see things differently.
💥 The undeniable proof that this work is **working**.

📩 **Email me:**
Hello@TheLotusBanks.com

📱 **Tag me on FB & Insta:**
@Lotus.Banks

🔥 You are so fucking beautiful. Keep going. I see you.

"When water seeks its own level, Be the wave."

— LOTUS BANKS

Level Fifteen

NOW WHAT?

You've come so far – disrupted old stories, rewired patterns, expanded your vision. Now you might be wondering, where the hell do I go from here?

Here's the deal: transformation isn't a one-and-done event; it's a lifelong journey. You've been the solution to your own struggles this entire time. You just needed the right tools to bring it out. And once you see what's possible, you can't unsee it. That's the **Law of Exposure**: Once you've tasted a higher level of awareness, you're never fully satisfied with your old limits again. You'll never <u>not know</u>, what you <u>now know</u>.

So, are you ready to **be the wave?**

When water seeks its own level, you can either sink to meet everyone else's comfort zone or rise up, challenging them to ascend alongside you.

Be the influence that inspires others to grow, rather than shrinking yourself to keep the peace. Because if you're serious about embodying your new level of awareness, healthy boundaries become essential.

Be the Wave
- A wave doesn't diminish itself to keep the rest of the water comfortable. It rises, and in doing so, *encourages* the rest to rise, too.
- You've built new patterns and rewired your thinking. Now it's time to **model** the changes you want to see in the world around you and the reality you experience.

Law of Exposure
- You can't "un-know" the things you've discovered about yourself. That means no more pretending you're okay with toxicity, or that your dreams are "too big."
- Don't let anyone talk you back into your old comfort zone. If others can't handle your growth, **that's their limitation**, not yours!

Boundaries
- "Boundaries are part of the responsibility of evolving," as my dad, an acupuncture physician and therapist, likes to say.
- As you change, you challenge other people's norms. Some might resist or even resent it, **especially** if they benefitted from your old unresourceful patterns.
- Protecting your emotional space is as crucial as locking your car doors or having a PIN on your bank account. Your mental well-being deserves just as much care.

How to embody, "When Water Seeks Its Own Level, Be The Wave. (And Hold The Line)":

Hold the Line
When pressure arises to revert to old habits, **remind yourself: stand firm now!** If someone tries to guilt-trip you or minimize your progress, politely but firmly decline to engage.

Invite Others to Rise
Don't just shut people out. Encourage them to join your new journey if they're willing. They might surprise you. If they won't? Accept that perhaps they've served their purpose in your story.

Celebrate Your Progress
Don't forget to reward yourself for reaching this point. By celebrating, you're telling your subconscious mind, "Yes, I want more of this!"

Continue the Journey
The real secret to lasting change is repetition. Revisit any of the previous levels or introspective exercises whenever you feel stuck or want a refresh. Check in with yourself regularly. In addition, I recommend going through all the levels once a year to continue to shift and expand even further.

Grow Your Sphere of Influence
Encourage friends, family, and coworkers to try these principles. Gift them a copy of this workbook for a holiday, birthday, or just because. Encourage your friends and family to follow me (and many other like-minded, growth-focused people) on social media, sign up for coaching or courses, and spread the word so we can all evolve together.

Imagine living in a world where everyone around you is equally committed to self-discovery and growth, a world where we each hold a higher standard for ourselves and those we love.

The wave you create by standing in your new power might just be the catalyst that inspires your closest allies, or even strangers, to level up, too.

That's the magic of real transformation: *it's contagious!*

So, what now? You keep going. You keep growing. You keep being the **wave** that refuses to settle and challenges others to rise.

Because once you know what you didn't know, there's no going back, and there's **only always**, another level.

Renegade Reflection:

You've done the work. You've seen what's possible. And the journey's just beginning. **Be the wave** that lifts the tide for everyone around you. Stand in your power, hold your boundaries, and remember: <u>you're the solution you've been searching for all along</u>. Embrace it. Own it. Live it.

Where might I still feel tempted to shrink myself for the comfort of others, and what would happen if I stopped?

_____
_____
_____
_____

Which boundaries do I most need to set/reinforce right now, and how can I communicate them clearly and from a loving space?

_____
_____
_____
_____
_____

How will I handle it when I outgrow certain relationships? What's my plan for parting ways or redefining those connections gracefully?

_____
_____
_____
_____
_____

What would the next level of personal evolution look like if I repeated these workbook levels once a year?

_____
_____
_____
_____

Renegade Unleashed!

This is it! The moment where **YOU** get to acknowledge the work, the breakthroughs, and the raw, unfiltered transformation you've just initiated. Take a deep breath, grab your pen, and let's make this real.

This isn't just about finishing a workbook. **This is about who you've become.**

What was the biggest bullshit story you shattered about yourself during this process, and how does it feel to no longer be owned by it?

_____
_____
_____
_____
_____

What's the one shift in your mindset that, once it clicked, changed everything for you?

_____
_____
_____
_____
_____

Which level challenged you the most, and what did it reveal about you that you hadn't seen before?

_____
_____
_____
_____
_____

What's one moment during this process where you realized you were more powerful than you thought?

_____
_____
_____
_____

If you could go back to the version of yourself that started this book, what advice would you give them now?

_____
_____
_____
_____
_____

What's the most undeniable evidence that you are not the same person who started this journey?

_____
_____
_____
_____
_____

What's the boldest, most unapologetic action you're committed to taking next to reinforce your growth?

_____
_____
_____
_____
_____

If your future self wrote a message to you right now, celebrating your evolution, what would they say?

_____
_____
_____
_____
_____

🔥 **YOU UNLEASHED YOURSELF – AND I WANT TO HEAR ALL ABOUT IT!** 🔥

You've done the work. You've disrupted, unraveled, and rewired. You've stepped into **the version of you that was always waiting beneath the surface.**

So, what now?

I want to hear it all: the breakthroughs, the breakdowns, the raw, unfiltered moments where you realized *holy shit, I'm different now.*

💥 What was your biggest shift?
💥 What old story did you finally burn to the ground?
💥 How are you showing up differently in your life now?

This isn't just about reflection, it's about *reinforcement!* When you speak your transformation into existence, you make it real.

So own it. Celebrate it. And share it with me.

📧 **Email me:**
Hello@TheLotusBanks.com

📲 **Tag me on FB & Insta:**
@Lotus.Banks

🔥 This is just the beginning. Keep rising.

Congratulations! 🔥

You. Fucking. Did. It.

You pushed past the excuses, shattered the old patterns, and claimed a new level of yourself that most people never even touch. Do you realize how rare that is? How many people buy a workbook, skim a few pages, and then let it collect dust?

Not you.

You showed up. You dug in. You disrupted the bullshit. And you refused to let your old story define your future. That's power. That's transformation. **That's being a renegade.**

Take a deep breath. Feel what you just did. **Let it sink in.**

Because now, you don't just *know* you're the solution, you **feel it.** You see it. You *own* it. And that? That changes *everything*.

Thank you for trusting me to guide you.

Thank you for being **bold, willing, and relentlessly seeking.**

And most of all, thank you for proving that…

When water seeks its own level, you choose to be the wave.

I love you immensely.

Now go celebrate the hell out of yourself!

Rising Always,

[signature]

Let's Connect!

What questions popped up for you while you worked through this book? What was your biggest "aha!" moment – or your biggest breakdown that led to an even bigger breakthrough? Now that you've caught a glimpse of your own badass potential, what's next?

I *seriously* want to know. Share your biggest takeaways, stories of transformation, or even your roadblocks. Tag me on social media or shoot me an email, and let's keep the conversation going.

- **Follow me on social** ➡ Facebook:    Instagram:
- **Email:** Hello@TheLotusBanks.com

Dive Deeper:
- **Live Mentorship + Courses:** Ready for more accountability, deeper strategies, and a thriving community that pushes you to grow? Join one of my programs today!
- **NLP Practitioner & Mindset Coaching Certification:** Interested in taking these tools to the next level, and helping others transform, too? Come train with me at my next certification event.
- **Scan code for details** ➡

Stay Connected & Level Up:
- **Freebies + Ongoing Support:** Sign up at www.TheLotusBanks.com to get exclusive resources and updates.
- **Free Facebook Community:** Join the disrupt-the-bullshit tribe (and invite all your friends too) for daily insights, inspiration, and real talk. Scan code ➡

Share the Love:
- **Write a Review:** If this workbook sparked transformation for you, drop a review and let the world know what's possible!
- **Become an Affiliate:** Want to earn $$ referring others to my coaching and courses? Let's partner up. Email me at Hello@TheLotusBanks.com for affiliate info.

Remember, your journey doesn't end here. Keep disrupting, keep evolving, and keep unleashing that inner renegade. I'll be cheering you on, and I can't wait to see what you create next!

Notes For Integration:

Notes For Integration:

Notes For Integration:

Notes For Integration:

Timeline Shift:

Objective: Find the root cause of a limiting decision and shift into an empowering belief.

Instructions:

1. State your limiting belief/decision:
   _____

2. Ask yourself, when did I decide that? (trust your gut, whatever comes up, go with it!)

3. On the horizontal timeline of your life below, mark the first time you recall this limiting belief, then mark key moments throughout your life that it was reinforced and got stronger.

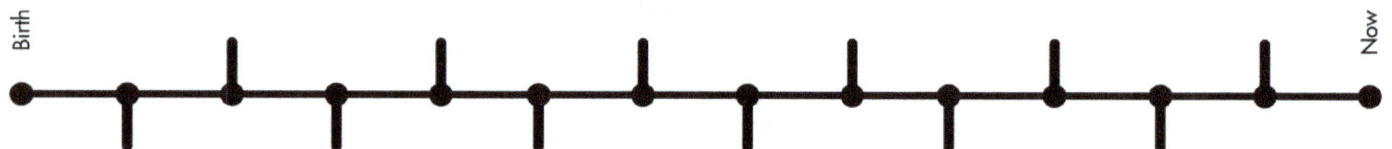

4. Ask yourself, "What do I need to learn from these events, the learnings which will allow me to release this old unresourceful belief easily and effortlessly?
   Write the answers below. Trust your subconscious response. No editing, no filtering. What do you need to LEARN so you can LET GO easily and effortlessly…
   _____
   _____

5. Ask yourself, "Where could I place a new decision, a new empowering belief on this timeline that changes the entire trajectory?" <u>Mark it in a different color or symbol!</u>

6. What are you choosing to believe instead? Write out your new empowering belief.
   _____
   _____

7. Close your eyes and picture yourself six months or a year from now, living fully aligned with your new belief. **Embody it.** Note your posture, facial expressions, how you speak.

8. Each day, find at least one piece of evidence that your new belief holds true…(Example: a small financial win if you're changing money beliefs, or a moment of trust in a relationship).

Timeline Shift:

Objective: Find the root cause of a limiting decision and shift into an empowering belief.

Instructions:

1. State your limiting belief/decision:

_____

2. Ask yourself, when did I decide that? (trust your gut, whatever comes up, go with it!)

3. On the horizontal timeline of your life below, mark the first time you recall this limiting belief, then mark key moments throughout your life that it was reinforced and got stronger.

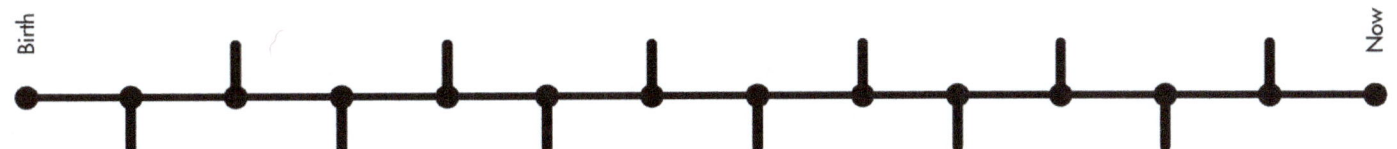

4. Ask yourself, "What do I need to learn from these events, the learnings which will allow me to release this old unresourceful belief easily and effortlessly?
   Write the answers below. Trust your subconscious response. No editing, no filtering. What do you need to LEARN so you can LET GO easily and effortlessly…

_____

_____

5. Ask yourself, "Where could I place a new decision, a new empowering belief on this timeline that changes the entire trajectory?" <u>Mark it in a different color or symbol!</u>

6. What are you choosing to believe instead? Write out your new empowering belief.

_____

_____

7. Close your eyes and picture yourself six months or a year from now, living fully aligned with your new belief. **Embody it.** Note your posture, facial expressions, how you speak.

8. Each day, find at least one piece of evidence that your new belief holds true…(Example: a small financial win if you're changing money beliefs, or a moment of trust in a relationship).

www.ingramcontent.com/pod-product-compliance
Lightning Source LLC
Chambersburg PA
CBHW080838230426
43665CB00021B/2883